The Essential Guide to Managing Corporate Crises

The Essential Guide to Managing Corporate Crises

A STEP-BY-STEP HANDBOOK

FOR SURVIVING MAJOR CATASTROPHES

Ian I. Mitroff

Christine M. Pearson

L. Katharine Harrington

New York Oxford | OXFORD UNIVERSITY PRESS | 1996

Oxford University Press

Oxford   New York
Athens   Auckland   Bangkok   Bombay
Calcutta   Cape Town   Dar es Salaam   Delhi
Florence   Hong Kong   Istanbul   Karachi
Kuala Lumpur   Madras   Madrid   Melbourne
Mexico City   Nairobi   Paris   Singapore
Taipei   Tokyo   Toronto

and associated companies in
Berlin   Ibadan

Library of Congress Cataloging-in-Publication Data
Mitroff, Ian I.
The essential guide to managing corporate crises :
a step-by-step handbook for surviving major catastrophes / Ian I. Mitroff.
Christine M. Pearson and L. Katharine Harrington.
p. cm.   Includes bibliographical references and index.
ISBN 0-19-509744-0
1. Crisis management.   I. Pearson, Christine M.   II. Harrington,
L. Katharine.   III. Title.
HD49.M573   1996
658.4—dc20   95-34628

1 3 5 7 9 8 6 4 2

Printed in the United States of America
on acid-free paper

PREFACE

This book is for those who need to know the essentials of crisis management, or CM. This includes all executives in key management positions, no matter what their job or function or the size or nature of their organization. It is intended also for those who work in the public or not-for-profit sector and those in the private or for-profit sector.

Two goals guided the writing and the organization of this book. First, the essentials of CM should be conveyed as clearly and directly as possible. Second, the book is intended to be used as a guide for managers before, during, and after a crisis.

Based on our experience in studying crises, teaching courses, and conducting seminars in CM; performing numerous pre- and postcrisis audits; and advising organizations during actual crises, we have concluded that most crisis manuals are useless. The reasons are as follows.

First, most manuals lack an overview of CM's systemic nature and, instead, present a variety of topics with little or no logical organization or framework to guide the user. For this reason, it is not surprising to find not only that most manuals are a source of confusion during a crisis but also that they actually enlarge the crisis.

Second, we are aware of no manual that covers all the relevant aspects or concerns associated with every crisis. Thus even if one is able to puzzle out the disorganization of most manuals, one is still not likely to find guidance in the many critical areas for which one is seeking help. This inadequacy only adds to the concern and confusion that accompany a crisis. Again, the tools intended to help managers deal with a crisis may become part of it.

Third, most CM manuals and programs contain either too much or too little detail. Some aspects of CM are covered in excruciating detail, whether or not they are critical, and others that are equally or even more important are ignored altogether or treated superficially.

Fourth, most manuals discuss only briefly the different concerns and perspectives that the members of a crisis management team (CMT) represent and need to raise during a crisis. Many manuals are created to satisfy the needs and/or anxieties of corporate headquarters, which helps explain why many manuals gloss over important issues and details. But this also means that when faced with an incident, executives and managers often find such sources difficult to sort through and lacking in sufficient detail to help them manage a crisis.

Fifth, most manuals do not give equal attention to what one needs to think about and do before, during, and after a crisis. Most manuals describe only what to do while a crisis is occurring. In this sense, they are primarily reactive. Based on our work with public and private organizations, we believe that CM manuals need to be proactive and retroactive as well. That is, they need to deal with issues before and after a crisis as much as those during a crisis.

Sixth and last, most CM manuals do not explain how an organization can ascertain whether it has the capability of carrying out the recommended plans and procedures. Any manual can make recommendations, but they will be useless if the organization cannot carry them out. Put differently, very few manuals specify the education, knowledge, and training required to implement an effective CM program. Fewer still tell the organization how to measure its performance. Any one of these defects can damage an organization's CM effectiveness, but all of them acting together can be fatal.

The purpose of this book is to give its users the necessary skills and understanding to deal with and manage crises before, during, and after they occur. Chapter 1 provides an overview of the entire CM process during a crisis. Chapter 2 offers a more detailed view of this same process. Chapters 3 and 4 examine what must be done before and after a crisis. Chapter 5 is an instruction manual for the CM software included with the book. It is a computerized version of Chapters 1 through 3. Using an example, Chapter 6 shows how a crisis should be handled. Finally, the seventh chapter summarizes what we have learned from dealing with crises and also the ideal management of a crisis.

This book assumes that the reader is not familiar with CM; that is, it is written for a broad professional audience. On the other hand, the book does assume that the reader has had some professional training and/or has worked in an organization, either private or public. In addition, this book is intended for both those facing their first crisis with little or no preparation and those wanting to improve their preparation and performance in time for their next crisis.

This book builds on our previous work in CM,[1] in particular, the crisis management recommendations developed by Mitroff, Pearson, and their associates.[2] Although our initial proposals addressed the concerns of practicing managers and executives, they were still too theoretical and did not provide detailed guidelines for actually managing crises. Rather, they identified the critical factors or dimensions. In contrast, this book discusses the key management actions and decisions that executives face in handling a crisis.

Those who are anxious to get started with the software CrMgt should turn directly to Chapter 5. We advise all readers to look at Chapter 5 whether or not they have a computer, as it presents a number of concepts and diagrams that are vital to understanding CM.

Los Angeles	I. I. M.
Chapel Hill	C. M. P.
Los Angeles	L. K. H.

NOTES

1. See Thierry C. Pauchant and Ian I. Mitroff, *Transforming the Crisis Prone Organization* (San Francisco: Jossey-Bass, 1992), and Ian I. Mitroff and Christine M. Pearson, *Crisis Management: A Diagnostic Guide for Improving Your Organization's Crisis-Preparedness* (San Francisco: Jossey-Bass, 1993).

2. Mitroff and Pearson, *Crisis Management*.

ABBREVIATED CONTENTS

CONTENTS

*Chapter 3 discusses precrisis auditing activities de-
signed to assess an organization's CM strengths and
vulnerabilities before a crisis occurs. It examines the
various types of crises that may occur, the phases
through which all crises pass, and the systems and
stakeholders that affect and are affected by a crisis.
The chapter includes a general audit guide to conducting a CM audit of an organization and a discussion of postcrisis analyses and how lessons from
previous crises can reduce future vulnerabilities.
Finally, this chapter addresses issues associated with
developing the capabilities to manage a crisis.*

*The ability to think systemically is necessary for
effective CM. Chapter 4 describes the roles and responsibilities of a CMT (team) and presents various
skill-building exercises to enable a CMT to function
effectively.*

*Chapter 5 is a guide to running CrMgt, the software
included with this book. It lists the hardware and
software requirements for loading and running
CrMgt and integrating CrMgt into the user's existing CM programs.*

*Chapter 6 uses an example to look at a particular
type of crisis, an industrial disaster. Since industrial
disasters may cause widespread destruction, it is important that we discuss at least one type of crisis in*

The Essential
Guide to
Managing
Corporate Crises

ONE

A Bird's-Eye View
of Crisis Management

WHAT TO DO WHEN A CRISIS HITS

This book has one overriding purpose, to present to executives the essentials of crisis management (CM) so that they and the organizations they manage can successfully weather a crisis. The book is also guided by the assumption that in today's world, it is not a question of if or whether an organization will experience a crisis; it is only a matter of what type of crisis will occur, what form it will take, and how and when it will happen.

Consider, for instance, 1993, a banner year for organizational crises: the shoot-out in Waco, Texas; the bombing of the World Trade Center in New York City; allegations of syringes in cans of Pepsi; deaths due to the consumption of Jack-in-the-Box burgers; kickbacks from Honda dealers to corporate executives; racial discrimination by Denny's restaurants. On and on it goes. It seems that hardly a day goes by without an organizational crisis occurring somewhere.

Some crises are inevitable no matter how well prepared an organization is, and indeed, complete prevention is not necessarily a goal of CM. In addition, as both a field of research and a corporate function, CM is still new and, as a result, is neither completely understood nor widely accepted at this point. Although more advanced and developed CM programs would not necessarily prevent all organizational crises from occurring, there is evidence that effective CM would enable most organizations to recover much faster and learn more from past crises.[1]

Based on our academic research and professional consultations,[2] we found the critical factor in determining how well an organization will perform during a crisis is how well prepared it is before the crisis occurs. For this reason, we cannot emphasize too strongly the importance of advance preparation.

One of the best ways to understand what you need to do before a crisis takes place is to understand what you need to do during its occurrence. Thus, even though effective performance during a crisis requires preparation before its occurrence, we will explain first what needs to be done during a crisis and then discuss what needs to be done beforehand. We will also talk about what needs to be done after a crisis has occurred so that you will be better prepared to handle future crises. (Make no mistake: Just as it is not a question of whether an organization will have a crisis, there is also little doubt that it will experience subsequent ones as well.)

There is another advantage to reversing the order of discussion. By first explaining what executives, managers, and organizations as a whole must do well during a crisis, we will better understand the capabilities that every organization should have in order to perform effectively. In other words, the best-formulated crisis plans, as well as the best abilities to "ad hoc it," will be useless if an organization does not have the capabilities required to handle a crisis. Indeed, an organization may actually be worse off if it substitutes a set of crisis plans and/or the ability to "think on its feet" for a competency in CM. Although plans and the ability to think and act quickly are certainly necessary and desirable qualities, neither is sufficient without the capability to carry it out. Such plans and ability also provide no assurance that an organization will perform well on all the aspects of CM.

WHAT IS A CRISIS?

There is no single, universally accepted, definition of a crisis, although there is general agreement that a crisis is an event that can destroy or affect an entire organization.[3] Accordingly, if something affects merely a part or one unit of an organization, it may or may not be, or lead to, a crisis.

A crisis can affect the very existence of an organization, a major product line, a business unit, or the like. A crisis also can damage, perhaps severely, an organization's financial performance. A crisis can also harm the health and well-being of consumers, employees, the surrounding community, and the environment itself. Finally, a crisis can destroy the public's basic trust or belief in an organization, its reputation, and its image.

A BIRD'S-EYE VIEW OF CM

We use diagrams frequently in this book to illustrate the CM skills and capabilities an organization needs in order to perform effectively. The diagrams are intended (1) to show the various actions, capabilities, and skills that effective CM requires; (2) to describe the components of these actions, capabilities, and skills; and (3) to relate them to one another so that as a particular action is performed, others can be anticipated. The diagrams thus are intended to give both "the big picture" and the details of CM. Some of the diagrams do one of the two, and others do both.

The Big Picture

Figure 1.1 is an overview of the actions and decisions that organizations must take during a crisis. It is not necessary at this point to understand in detail every part of Figure 1.1, but by the end of the chapter you should have a general understanding of it.

Box 1: The Precipitating Crisis

Regardless of the way in which its occurrence has come to your attention, your organization has been hit by a crisis, as shown in Box 1 of Figure 1.1. The crisis may be a major (1) threat to your organization's credibility, identity, or reputation; (2) financial disaster; (3) health threat to consumers, employees, or surrounding community; (4) class-action suit; (5) sabotage attempt; (6) product defect; (7) tampering incident; or (fill in the blank).

Box 2: Anticipating and Managing the Media

A crisis sets in motion two distinct activities that must be managed simultaneously: responding to the crisis itself and responding to the media. If the crisis is se-

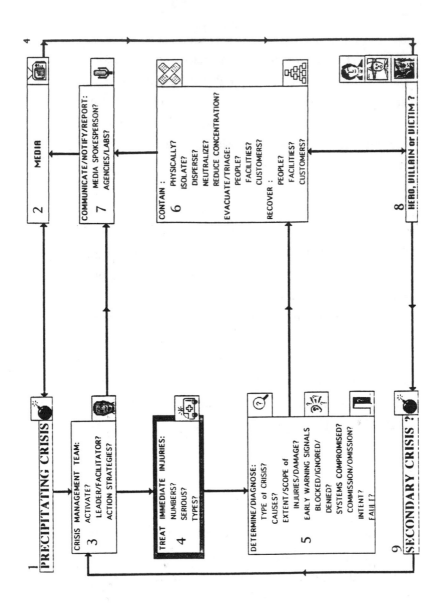

1 PRECIPITATING CRISIS

2 MEDIA

3 CRISIS MANAGEMENT TEAM:
ACTIVATE?
LEADER/FACILITATOR?
ACTION STRATEGIES?

4 TREAT IMMEDIATE INJURIES:
NUMBERS?
SERIOUS?
TYPES?

5 DETERMINE/DIAGNOSE:
TYPE of CRISIS?
CAUSES?
EXTENT/SCOPE of
INJURIES/DAMAGE?
EARLY WARNING SIGNALS
BLOCKED/IGNORED/
DENIED?
SYSTEMS COMPROMISED?
COMMISSION/OMISSION?
INTENT?
FAULT?

6 CONTAIN :
PHYSICALLY?
ISOLATE?
DISPERSE?
NEUTRALIZE?
REDUCE CONCENTRATION?
EVACUATE/TRIAGE:
PEOPLE?
FACILITIES?
CUSTOMERS?
RECOVER :
PEOPLE?
FACILITIES?
CUSTOMERS?

7 COMMUNICATE/NOTIFY/REPORT:
MEDIA SPOKESPERSON?
AGENCIES/LABS?

8 HERO, VILLAIN or VICTIM ?

9 SECONDARY CRISIS ?

rious, the media will be involved in its coverage from the very beginning. In some cases, media coverage may even escalate the crisis itself. (For this reason, there is an arrow from the media, Box 2, to the precipitating crisis, Box 1.)

The media will certainly be interested and involved in the unfolding and handling of a crisis. Thus, from the start, you must have a strategy and a capability for managing the issues that the media will invariably raise. This does not mean that crisis communications are thereby the principal or the most essential aspect of CM, as many PR (public relations) consultants would have managers believe. Of course, the ability to anticipate and respond effectively to the media is a very important aspect of all crises; in some cases, it is the most important aspect. But effective crisis communications are not the only important aspect of all crises. Other skills and capabilities are necessary to manage a crisis.

The questions that the media will ask during a crisis probably will include the following:

1. Is the crisis your organization's fault, and if not, how do you know that it is not?

2. What is your organization doing about the situation, whether or not it is at fault, and especially if it is?

Figure 1.1. A bird's-eye view of crisis management.

3. When did your organization first learn about the situation, and what did it then do?

4. Were there any warning signals that such a crisis might occur, and if there were, what actions did your organization take when it first learned about the situation, to prevent it from occurring?

5. If warning signals were not detected or if the organization did not take any actions, why not?

Box 3: Should Your Organization's Crisis Management Team Be Activated?

If a crisis is indeed serious or appears to be, then the company's crisis management team (CMT) should be activated immediately. This recommendation assumes, of course, that the company has a CMT and, furthermore, that it is well trained and prepared.

Ideally, a CMT should be made up of executives and managers with various backgrounds and roles. In short, the team needs the skills and training to handle the multiple concerns and problems that every crisis creates. Most CMTs have representatives from the following departments: (1) legal, (2) finance, (3) operations, (4) security, (5) public affairs or public relations, (6) health and safety, and (7) human relations. Other functions and skills can be brought in as needed to manage the particular crisis at hand.

One thing is clear: Given the diverse makeup that a CMT requires, advance training is necessary so that team members can learn to balance and integrate their various perspectives. For instance, lawyers typically want to say as little as possible during a crisis in order to avoid or minimize legal liability. Marketing, public affairs, and public relations executives, on the other hand, want to share information more broadly as a means of retaining or recovering consumer confidence and hence safeguarding their business. Dissent and interpersonal tension can result from such fundamentally different views. A crisis, furthermore, is one of the worst possible times to iron out these inevitable disagreements among different roles and perspectives.

Box 4: Helping the Injured
Is Priority Number One

If we had to choose the number-one priority in all crises, it would be the prompt treatment of injuries to humans, animals, and the environment. This necessitates knowing the numbers and types of injuries or damages, if any. It certainly is not acceptable to respond with either arrogance or contempt, as the chairman of Exxon, Lawrence Rawl, did regarding the oil spill in Prince William Sound, near Valdez, Alaska:

> I've been with Exxon for thirty-eight years, and the thing that has bothered me most is not the castigation, the difficulties or the long hours; it's been the embarrassment. I hate to be embarrassed, and I am. Our safety practices have been excellent, and we have drilled them and drilled them into our employees over the decades. There is a lot of pride inside Exxon all over the world, and that pride is being challenged. We'll win it back, but we are not going to do it by debating on TV with some guy who says, "You know, you killed a number of birds." And we say, "We're sorry, we're doing all we can." There were thirty million birds that went through the sound last summer, and only 30,000 carcasses have been recovered. Just look at how many ducks are killed in the Mississippi delta in one hunting day in December! People have come up to me and said, "This is worse than Bhopal." I say, "Hell, Bhopal killed more than three thousand people and injured two hundred thousand others!" Then they say, "Well, if you leave the people out, it was worse than Bhopal."[4]

An article in *Fortune* put the matter even more bluntly in criticizing Rawl:

Where Exxon looks chiefly vulnerable is in leadership. Rawl and his team appear to lack the ability to understand people and to inspire them. Management has repeatedly underestimated public reaction to the spill and contrives to talk as though the public has nothing at stake. Rawl says he didn't go to Alaska at once because the clean-up was in capable hands and he had "many other things to do." An interesting point here: the earnings of his U.S. operations were going down the drain in Prince William Sound, yet he didn't rush to the site.

By going to Alaska and acquitting himself while in the spotlight, Rawl would have accomplished two purposes: He would have reassured the public that the people who run Exxon acknowledge their misdeed and would make amends. And he might have salvaged the pride that Exxon workers once had in their company. Says one manager: "Wherever I travel now, I feel like I have a target painted on my chest. Employees are confused, embarrassed, and betrayed. Says an executive working in New Jersey: "The company is in turmoil. It is hard to get decisions. Everyone is studying safety in addition to his normal responsibilities."[5]

We cannot emphasize too strongly that an organization's primary concern should not be merely the establishment of the numbers and extent of injuries but a prompt, effective, and humane response. This, in turn, requires that an organization be able either to send emergency medical response teams immediately to any site worldwide or to activate local, on-site teams.

If we have learned anything from studying countless crises,[6] it is that the inability to handle well the initial crisis can set off a chain reaction of additional crises far worse than the first one. The key to whether an organization will be perceived (Box 8) as a hero, victim, or villain is its ability to respond quickly with genuine care and concern. We are the first to admit that this is often easier to say than to do, even if your organization is caring and wants to do the right thing. The difficulty is that a paradox is often associated with prompt and effective caring treatment. That is, prompt treatment can sometimes be ineffective, even wrong, and effective treatment sometimes means delayed treatment.

Box 5: What Is the Crisis?

You may well assume that an organization would "know" what the initial precipitating crisis is, but more often than not, it does not. In many situations, what the organization "knows" is what someone "thinks" the initial or precipitating crisis is. Box 5 lists several *detective actions* designed to identify the precise nature of the crisis, including (1) the exact nature or type of the crisis, (2) whether there were any early warning signals associated with the crisis, and (3) the causes of the crisis. The knowledge gained from such detective actions is invaluable in treating the crisis.

Box 6: Containing the Damage and Recovering

The containment activities show in Box 6 extend the set of treatment actions. Two activities are especially important here: damage containment and recovery. Damage containment means putting into action specific mechanisms designed to keep a particular crisis from spreading or contaminating other, unaffected parts of an organization. For example, firewalls help keep a fire in one part of a building from spreading to other parts. One reasons that we need to know the precise type of a particular crisis is that different crises require different damage containment mechanisms and procedures. For example, damage mechanisms to contain a product-tampering incident generally differ from those needed to contain a toxic chemical spill or damage to a corporation's reputation.

In the same way, different crises also call for different business recovery strategies. For instance, can you safely resume producing a damaged brand? Is it safe to reenter buildings or to allow citizens to return to their community? Can you recover manufacturing operations, distribution channels, and the like? Can an organization's reputation be reinstated? Do you have backup computers to safeguard key information? Do you have backup manufacturing and management sites? These are only a few of the critical issues associated with business recovery.

Box 7: Communicating to the Media and the Authorities

What you have learned about the nature of the crisis, its treatment, and its recovery will affect what you can communicate to the media and the appropriate governmental, health, and police agencies. Even though you must start communicating immediately with the media (as represented by the horizontal line to the right of Box 1), you must also update and revise what you say in light of ongoing investigations and treatment.

CM is a dynamic process. Honest and open communication with the authorities and the media does not require perfect, instantaneous knowledge. Furthermore, although every attempt should be made to ensure that communication is accurate, the spokesperson should avoid speculation. Initial statements and actions can be revised as more is learned. There is nothing wrong with saying at the outset, "We don't know exactly what happened, but I promise we will get back to you as soon as we do know more."

Boxes 8 and 9: Will Your Organization Be a Hero, Victim, or Villain?

How your organization performs on every aspect of the CM process outlined in Figure 1.1 will determine in the end whether the media and the public perceive the organization favorably as a hero or a victim or unfavorably as a villain. The mismanagement of a crisis is one of the surest ways in which to earn the label *villain*. If mismanaged, virtually all crises lead to a secondary, and potentially worse, crisis (Box 9) and usually result in long-term damage to the organization's reputation.

THE SYSTEMIC NATURE OF CM

Effective CM is systemic,[7] which means that it is the product of or the interaction among all the critical activities represented in Figure 1.1. Effective CM is not a function of how well an organization does on one part of Figure 1.1 in isolation from the others, and it is not the sum of separate activities. In this sense, $1 + 1 = 2$ does not apply to CM. Rather, effective CM is more akin to the product of 1×1. If an organization does well on one critical activity (and thus earns a score of 1) but does poorly on some other activity (and thus scores 0), its overall performance will be represented by $1 \times 0 = 0$! In a crisis, poor performance in one area is not compensated by exceptional performance in another.

CONCLUDING REMARKS

Let us summarize what we have covered thus far, in the form of a series of questions that all executives and their organizations need to address. (These questions are listed in Table 1.1 for you to score with regard to your organization.) First, does your organization have the necessary abilities to assess the potential numbers and types of injuries that can be associated with any crisis? Does your organization have the capabilities required to treat whatever injuries might result? Does your organization's value system or culture give priority to treating injuries promptly? Or does it give priority to covering up or denying a crisis? Do legal considerations override ethical and human concerns? Does your organization have a trained crisis management team (CMT) that can assemble quickly and make effective decisions? Does your organization have the capabilities to investigate and determine (1) the precise type or nature of the crises that could occur; (2) the early warning signals that precede each type of crisis; (3) whether such signals were blocked or ignored; and (4) the exact human, organizational, and technical causes of a potential crisis? Does your organization have properly designed, constantly maintained, and regularly tested damage containment systems in place? Does your organization have backup manufacturing sites and computers so that it can resume operations as quickly as possible? Does it have recovery mechanisms to restore full site and corporate operations? Does it have recovery mechanisms to restore the surrounding community and the environment? Does it have the capabilities to communicate effectively and notify the proper authorities, respond to the media, and reassure a wide array of stakeholders?

A helpful rule to bear in mind is that there are no secrets in CM. In the event of a crisis, your organization's responses to each of the preceding questions and issues not only will be discovered but also will most likely be publicized. As a result, your ability to respond will become the grounds on which your organization will be judged. In addition, your strengths and weaknesses will be investigated repeatedly and

TABLE 1.1. HOW WELL PREPARED IS YOUR ORGANIZATION FOR A CRISIS?

Statement	Yes	No
1. Our organization has the necessary abilities to assess the potential numbers and types of injuries associated with any crisis.	_____	_____
2. Our organization has the capabilities required to treat whatever injuries might result.	_____	_____
3. Our organization's value system or culture gives priority to treating injuries promptly.	_____	_____
4. Our organization gives priority to covering up or denying a crisis.	_____	_____
5. Legal considerations do not override ethical and human concerns.	_____	_____
6. Our organization has a trained crisis management team (CMT) that can assemble quickly and make effective decisions.	_____	_____
7. Our organization has the capabilities to investigate and determine		
a. the precise type or nature of whatever crisis could occur.	_____	_____
b. the early warning signals that precede each type of crisis.	_____	_____
c. whether such signals were blocked or ignored.	_____	_____

TABLE 1.1. (continued)

d. the exact human,
organizational, and technical
causes of a crisis.   _____ _____

8. Our organization has properly
designed, constantly maintained,
and regularly tested damage
containment systems in place.   _____ _____

9. Our organization has backup
manufacturing sites and computers
so that it can resume operations as
quickly as possible.   _____ _____

10. Our organization has recovery
mechanisms to restore full site and
corporate operations.   _____ _____

11. Our organization has recovery
mechanisms to restore the surrounding community and the
environment.   _____ _____

12. Our organization has the capabilities to communicate effectively,
notify the proper authorities,
respond to the media, and reassure
a wide array of stakeholders.   _____ _____

If you answered no to two or more of these statements, it is likely not only that your organization will have a crisis but also that it will have difficulty handling it properly.

magnified for all to see, especially on the front pages of national newspapers and the opening minutes of national newscasts.

Notes

1. Thierry C. Pauchant and Ian I. Mitroff, *Transforming the Crisis Prone Organization* (San Francisco: Jossey-Bass, 1992).

2. Ibid.

3. Ibid. See also Charles Perrow, *Normal Accidents: Living with High Risk Technologies* (New York: Basic Books, 1984).

4. Quoted in Richard Behar, "Exxon Strikes Back," *Time*, March 26, 1990, p. 63.

5. Peter Nulty, "Exxon's Problem: Not What You Think, the Embattled Oil Giant Is in Good Enough Financial Shape That It Can Almost Shrug off the Cost of the Alaskan Clean Up. But Morale and Long Term Leadership Are Another Matter," *Fortune*, April 23, 1990, p. 204.

6. See Pauchant and Mitroff, *Transforming the Crisis Prone Organization*.

7. For an in-depth discussion of systems and systems thinking, see Ian I. Mitroff and Harold Linstone, *The Unbounded Mind* (New York: Oxford University Press, 1993); see also Russell L. Ackoff, *The Democratic Organization, a Radical Prescription Recreating Corporate America and Rediscovering Success* (New York: Oxford University Press, 1994).

TWO

What to Do
During a Crisis

A DETAILED GUIDE

Chapter 1 presented an overview of the actions that executives need to take during a crisis, the issues they need to address, and the relationship among these activities and issues. This relationship is important because in a crisis they need not only to attend to those issues requiring immediate attention but also to anticipate how their immediate actions will affect future actions. All the activities and decisions listed in Figure 1.1 are tightly intertwined and hence affect one another. For this reason, we believe that effective CM depends on how well an organization performs all the activities in Figure 1.1, and not on just one or two of them in isolation.

In this chapter, we will explore in more detail each of the boxes in Figure 1.1. To do this, we will use other figures that seem different from Figure 1.1. As before, we will both examine the activities and decisions one at a time and show them in relationship to one another so that as you are performing one activity, you can plan for those following it.

THE INITIAL INFORMATION AND ACTION PHASE OF CM

The First Point of Contact: The Accuracy, Credibility, and Power of the Initial Sources of Information

Figure 2.1 illustrates the beginning phase of CM, how a crisis comes to an organization's attention. Box 1 of this figure indicates that a crisis can be brought to an organization's attention by either internal or external sources or some combination of the two.

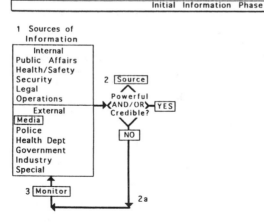

Figure 2.1. The first decision: finding out how a crisis comes to an organization's attention.

The first critical decision that every organization must make pertains to the power and/or credibility of the source bringing the crisis to its attention. (In all the following figures, a critical decision is enclosed in a diamond, and the outcomes of decisions or activities are in rectangles.) If the source is judged to be neither powerful nor credible (the "no" box just below Diamond 2 in Figure 2.1), the organization is advised to monitor (Point 3) the situation carefully in order to determine whether the initial information is an early warning signal of an impending crisis.

Determining the power and credibility of an information source is obviously a judgment call, as are most of the decisions required in CM, and so they depend on the experience, knowledge, and skills of the person or persons monitoring the incoming information. This does not mean that there are no sound bases on which to make the initial decisions with regard to a source's power and/or credibility. Indeed, such judgments are likely to be based on the experience and expertise of relevant members of the organization. For example, a call from *60 Minutes* or *Nightline* should be considered important (i.e., powerful), no matter what its credibility. By definition, inquiries from any major national publication should also be taken very seriously. The point is that the initial phase of CM invariably involves judgments with regard to the potential seriousness of a situation.

Since the notion of "power" is essential here, we should say a bit more about its definition. An example of the traditional definition of power is that person A is said to have power over person B if A can force B to perform actions that on his or her own, B would not perform. More generally, A is said to have power over B if A can "influence" B's behavior. This definition applies to CM as well, but another, more important definition also applies: One person or, more generally, one stakeholder, A, has power over another stakeholder, B, if A can cause a noncrisis situation to become a crisis for B. According to this definition, the news media certainly have power, and therefore a call from a representative of a major news organization should be taken very seriously. Indeed, the call itself should be regarded as a "potential crisis," and not merely an "incoming message."

On the other hand, a call or action by one of the major news media does not mean that an organization should automatically admit guilt. In some cases, it should contest allegations of wrongdoing. A classic example is NBC's showing GM trucks catching fire: GM successfully contested the charges and proved that NBC had deliberately tampered with GM's products to produce the story. As with the earlier definition of power, we can say that one expert, A, is more credible than another, B, if A can force an organization into a crisis situation.

To Be or Not to Be Proactive

If a source is deemed to be powerful and/or credible, the next critical decision an organization faces is whether or not it should be "proactive." Should the organization move into an active crisis response mode *before* the full extent of damage or injuries (if any) can be established? In many cases, regardless of whether or not the organization is responsible for any damage or injuries, being proactive can be a real plus. That is, the organization will have acted responsibly on its own without being prodded by other forces or agencies. The risk, of course, is that quick actions may not only be ill conceived but also may imply guilt. In some cases, quick actions may also cost an organization sizable amounts of money or other resources. Yet in many cases, organizations report winning generous amounts of goodwill for their early actions.

Once an organization decides to be proactive, the next critical decision (Figure 2.2, Point 5) is whether it is prepared for CM. The decision in this case is not whether the organization "determines" at this time that it is prepared to handle a crisis but whether the actions it has taken in the past have prepared it to handle a crisis.

If the organization is proactive (Point 4a) and is prepared for CM, its first action should be to activate its crisis management team (CMT) (Point 6). On

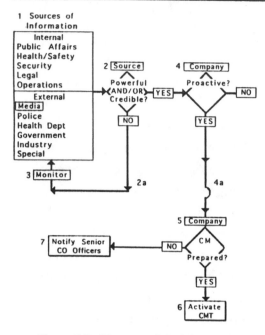

Figure 2.2. The second decision: whether an organization is prepared for CM.

the other hand, if the organization is not prepared for CM, each of its senior officers (Point 7) must be notified immediately.

There is a vicious paradox associated with not being prepared: If an organization is ill prepared, then it is unlikely that its senior officers will be notified in a timely fashion, if at all. One of the noticeable characteristics of organizations that are not well prepared is that they do not convey important information from one part of the organization to others, for reasons that we shall examine in more detail later.[1]

To Assume or
Not to Assume Responsibility?

Figure 2.3 shows the next series of critical CM activities and decisions. One characteristic of CM- prepared organizations (the "yes" box preceding Point 6) is that they are ready to assume responsibility for a crisis before they know all the particulars of the case at hand (e.g., the full extent of injuries and whether or not the organization is responsible for them). As a general rule, CM-prepared organizations assume responsibility (Point 9) even when they are not responsible.[2] This does not mean that they are pushovers that accept responsibility for everything (Point 8); rather, it means that concern for their consumers, employees, the general public, and the environment is valued over immediate, short-term profits. (Johnson & Johnson's handling of the Tylenol poisonings is an excellent example of this kind of behavior.[3])

CM-prepared organizations understand implicitly that concern for people and the environment is vital to their continued existence and hence to their long-term profits. For this reason, at the very first sign of a crisis, they commence a coordinated crisis response

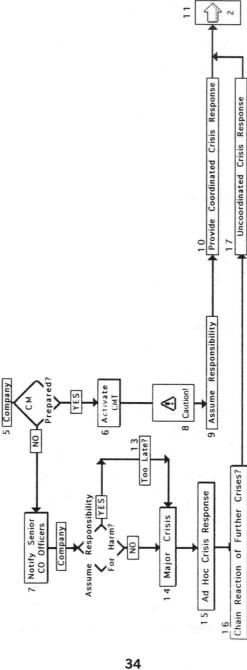

Figure 2.3. The third decision: whether an organization is prepared to assume responsibility for a crisis.

34

(Point 10). As soon as possible, a member of their CMT is sent to the site of the crisis to begin fact-finding and to coordinate recovery and treatment activities. CM-prepared organizations also are able to enhance their response by mobilizing their crisis command centers. They call important external stakeholders such as government agencies, research contract labs, and other firms that can provide specialized CM expertise. Such organizations have developed and tested all the relevant contacts far in advance so that they do not have to scramble to make those contacts during a crisis.

Figure 2.3 also shows the kind of scrambling required by a CM-unprepared organization. Even if it assumes responsibility for harm (Point 13), it may be delayed or too late. If the organization has caused harm and does not assume responsibility (Point 14), then its lack of preparation will become part of the crisis itself (Point 15), as it will compound its errors (Point 16) by virtue of its ad hoc and uncoordinated crisis responses (Point 17). All this will result in a chain reaction of further crises (Point 16) that bring additional uncoordinated crisis responses (Point 17).

Seriousness and Responsibility

Figure 2.4 shows the series of decisions and activities that will be needed if an organization decides not

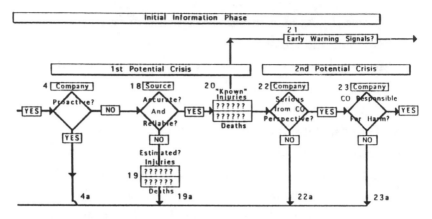

Figure 2.4. The fourth decision: determining the seriousness of a crisis and the organization's responsibility for it.

to be proactive (the "no" decision box to the immediate right of Diamond 4; see also Figure 2.2). In this case, the decision to act is deferred until more accurate and reliable numbers are collected regarding the extent and seriousness of injuries (Point 22). If the available numbers are deemed inaccurate and unreliable (Point 19a), the situation should be monitored for further developments (Figure 2.1, Point 3). If the numbers are believed to be reasonably accurate and reliable and hence "known" (Point 20), questions (Points 22 and 23) should be asked about (1) the seriousness of the crisis from the company's point of view and (2) whether or not the company is responsible for the crisis.

Note that in reality, there are far too many decision loops to show each of them here. For instance, even if the available numbers (Diamond 18) are not deemed accurate or reliable, the organization may still decide to proceed (Diamond 22) because it feels the situation may be important and so may decide to dispatch a member of its CMT, or another top executive, to examine the situation more closely.

The determinations of seriousness and responsibility naturally raise the important issue of what the criteria are that should influence an organization to accept responsibility and act. Although there is no one answer to this problem, we can offer some guidelines. Table 2.1 shows the criteria used by two very different organizations with whom we have worked that should trigger a crisis response. The left-hand column pertains to a company in the chemical industry, and the right-hand one, to one in the food industry.

In effect, the criteria constitute a threshold. If an event meets or exceeds any of the criteria listed in each row of the table, the company should act decisively. Note that although there are distinct differences between the two sets, there is nonetheless a remarkable degree of overlap between them. The criteria are thus broadly applicable to organizations no matter what their business.

TABLE 2.1. CRITERIA/EVENTS THAT WILL TRIGGER A CRISIS RESPONSE

Industrial Crisis	Food-Related Crisis	Your Organization
1. Affects the outside community or environment: The incident closes major major roads or public facilities.	1. One serious consumer injury.	1._____ _____ _____ _____
2. Causes fatalities (one or more).	2. Two complaints of illness or injury with regard to the same product/code.	2._____ _____
3. Causes multiple injuries or exposure to a serious chemical hazard.	3. Likelihood of recall or withdrawal.	3._____ _____
4. Releases known carcinogens or toxic materials even if they are contained in a sealed-off area.	4. Media or agency involvement.	4._____ _____ _____ _____
5. Draws media attention from the outside.	5. Tampering or a threat of tampering.	5._____ _____
6. Enters a waterway.	6. Serious injury involving facility or employees.	6._____ _____
7. Forces a master shutdown or complete evacuation of facilities, thereby attracting media attention.	7. Facility explosion or fire.	7._____ _____ _____

TABLE 2.1. (continued)

Industrial Crisis	Food-Related Crisis	Your Organization
8. Is of sufficient magnitude to require regulatory notification.	8. Bomb threat, kidnapping.	8. _____ _____
9. Shuts down an operating unit.	9. Facility evacuation.	9. _____
10. Is a repetition of similar events.	10. Spill or leak.	10. _____
11. Has an extended duration of more than five hours.	11. Serious property damage to facility caused by weather or violence.	11. _____ _____
12. Is any special circumstance that might escalate the event/issue.	12. Strike/walkout at facility.	12. _____ _____
	13. Health/safety problems at facility.	13. _____
	14. Civil unrest near facility.	14. _____
	15. Media attention.	15. _____

Delayed Response

Figure 2.5 shows the full set and sequence of critical decisions and activities that comprise the initial information-gathering and action phases of CM. It shows that the precipitating crisis can lead to several more crises (the first, second, third, and fourth potential crisis phases), depending on how the organization responds or is perceived to respond. Figure 2.5 shows that if the response to the initial crisis is delayed too long in order to collect sufficiently accurate and reliable numbers (Point 24) and if the company is not prepared for CM, the delay itself can further fuel the initial crisis (Point 13).

One of the most important lessons to be learned from the way in which crises unfold is that every organization needs to formulate criteria for action that are specially suited to its situation. The criteria are essential to helping determine which direction to move in as the organization proceeds through Figure 2.5. Of course, we can offer only general guidelines for your organization to consider.

Figure 2.5 shows the kinds of issues you should consider during a crisis and also, ideally, before one occurs. After you have studied the figure, you can begin to appreciate why CM requires preparation

---

Figure 2.5. The fifth decision: making the initial information-gathering and action decisions.

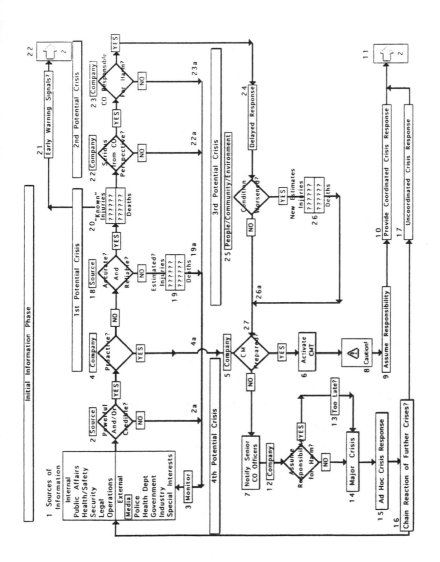

41

before a crisis. There are too many issues and activities occurring throughout the process of Figure 2.5 to "ad hoc it." Unprepared companies can expect some dissension and infighting, which only will intensify the crisis. This may be true even of those organizations that are somewhat CM prepared, since every crisis unleashes powerful emotions.[4] Typically, in unprepared organizations, untrained senior officers can be expected to retreat to their specialized training and their usual ways of reacting to stress.

DIAGNOSING THE CRISIS

What Is the Crisis?

Figure 2.6 shows the next series of critical activities and decisions making up the second major part of the CM process. Despite whether an organization is prepared for CM (Figure 2.5, Point 6) or not (Figure 2.5, Point 27), and hence executes a coordinated or uncoordinated crisis response, the precise type and nature of the crisis must be determined.

There are eleven basic types of crises, ranging from criminal attacks to punitive regulatory legislation. (We will examine the various subtypes of these eleven basic types in more detail later.) In addition, though they are distinct, these basic types are neither exhaustive nor exclusive. Because of its complexity,

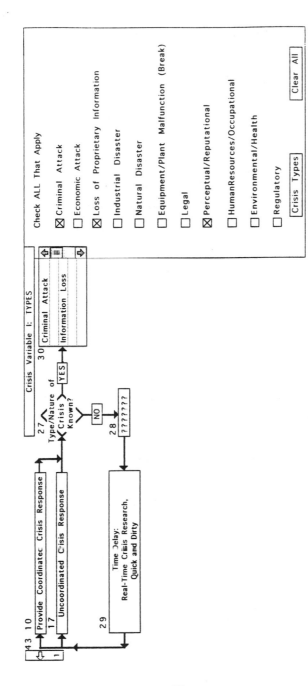

Figure 2.6. The sixth decision: determining the type of crisis.

43

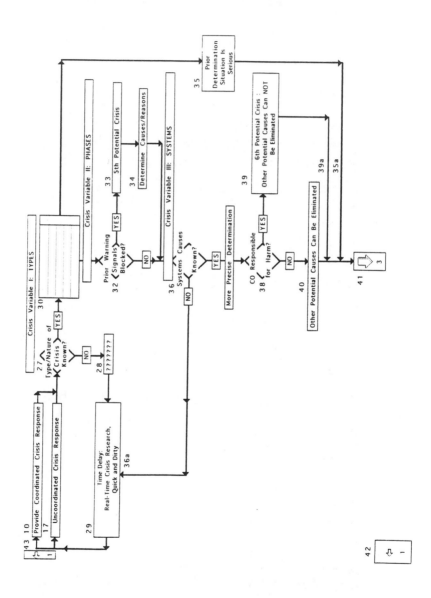

44

a crisis may fall into one or more types at the same time, depending on the circumstances, and any one of the types in Figure 2.6 is capable of causing any other type. That is, any of the types can be the cause and/or the effect of any other.[5]

A crisis's precise nature or type may not always be immediately apparent, which is one of the best reasons for not taking immediate or drastic action until the nature and extent of injuries have been determined (Figure 2.5, Point 20). Moreover, if your organization is crisis prepared, when you begin determining the numbers of injuries, you should also begin determining the type of crisis that produced the injuries. In other words, identifying a crisis and determining whether injuries have resulted are complementary acts; they should not be viewed as separate activities. This is a strong justification for considering the set of crisis activities and decisions as an integrated whole. When you take a particular action or decision, you should be thinking how it will influence others.

Figure 2.8 shows that if you do not know (as indicated by the giant question marks) the "type" of a crisis (Figure 2.7, Point 28), you will lose time (Point 29) finding out. The activities in Figure 2.7, Box 29,

---

Figure 2.7. The seventh decision: deciding on an organization's CM preparation and response.

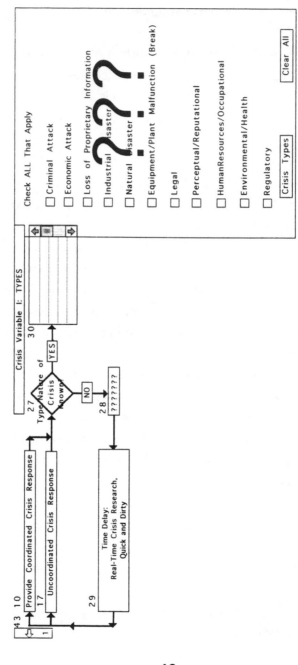

Figure 2.8. Why not being prepared loses time.

46

are critical because further actions and decisions presuppose some knowledge, however sketchy, of the crisis's type.

Point 32 in Figure 2.7 asks whether any early warning signals associated with the crisis were blocked or not transmitted in the appropriate language to the appropriate person at the appropriate place and time in the organization. One of the most important findings in CM is that with very few exceptions, crises send out a trail of early warning signals before their actual occurrence.[6] If such signals can be detected, many crises can be prevented from occurring—the best possible form of CM. If the signals associated with a crisis were blocked, then finding out what the particular kinds of blocks were can help prevent future crises. But once a crisis has occurred and an organization is under the magnifying lens of the media, there can be few secrets. Indeed, it is likely that the fact that early warning signals were blocked will be revealed, and so become part of the crisis itself. For this reason, it is important to know whether any early warning signs were present and how they were handled. For instance, one of the biggest contributing factors to the explosion of the *Challenger* was the fact that messages warning of the potentially unsafe condition of the O-rings were prevented from reaching those at the top of NASA's hierarchy.[7]

In a similar manner, those activites occurring in Crisis Variable III, SYSTEMS (Figure 2.7, Point 36) encompass a whole set of investigative actions designed to uncover the causes of a crisis. If the causes are not known (Point 36a), a "quick and dirty" investigation to determine the crisis's causes will be necessary.

The following factors have been shown to be present in every crisis: (1) technology, (2) human factors, (3) organizational structure, (4) culture, and (5) top management psychology. Most organizations have core technologies that are closely linked to the production of their key products and services. For instance, certain chemical processes constitute the core technology of a chemical refinery. Computers are one of the most vulnerable technologies of virtually every organization.

A second cause of organizational crises is "human factors." All technologies are operated by people who cannot be presumed to be infallible. Operators often make errors, with job overload and stress increasing that probability. Thus, the possible human causes of every crisis must be examined.

If technologies could exist and operate on their own, we might not have crises; unfortunately, however, technologies and people are interdependent. Power, authority, and egos often get in the way of safe operations when organizations conceal vital information. A recurring question in trying to determine the cause of a crisis is whether an organization's channels of communication have been blocked. If so, how did this contribute to the crisis? Did the organization's reward system contribute as well? For instance, is getting products out the door valued more highly than safety? These are only a few of the questions to ask about the potential contributions of organizational factors to crises.

An organization's culture has also been found to be a principal cause of many crises. Indeed, certain organizations are labeled *crisis prone*.[8] Such organizations embody attitudes that almost guarantee a crisis. That is, they use rationalizations (e.g., "We're so big and powerful that nothing bad can happen to us") to deny their need for advanced CM planning and preparation. At the other extreme, a much smaller number of organizations are *crisis prepared*.

Finally, the attitudes and values of top executives have been found to be strong contributing factors. If an organization's managers believe that they and their organizations are invulnerable, a crisis is much more likely.

All these factors (Figure 2.7, Point 38) affect whether or not an organization is responsible for harm. Only when all other factors or explanations can be eliminated (Point 40) can we say for sure that the organization was or was not responsible. The facts uncovered by the investigations (Points 32, 36, and 38) are thus critical, as they determine subsequent actions to (1) contain the crisis, (2) treat it, (3) communicate to the authorities and other important stakeholders, and (4) learn from the crisis.

TREATING THE CRISIS

Containment and Treatment

Figure 2.9 shows why knowing the particular type of a crisis and its specific causes is important. When you do not have such knowledge, it is very difficult to contain the crisis and treat its full effects, and you do not know which containment and treatment options are best.

The five basic types of containment and treatment options are (1) isolation, (2) removal, (3) dispersal, (4) reduction, and (5) neutralization. First, for isolation, we physically or psychologically separate—or attempt to separate—the crisis from the organization. For instance, in the case of a toxic or hazardous spill, we put a physical barrier around the spill area to contain and isolate it from the rest of an organization or community. In the case of a political or

Figure 2.9. The eighth decision: deciding on containment and treatment.

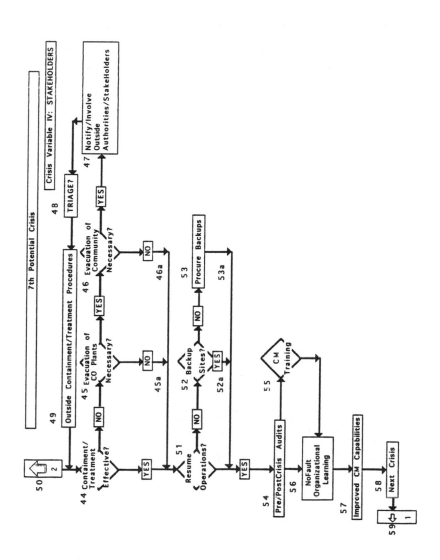

7th Potential Crisis

Crisis Variable IV: STAKEHOLDERS

48 TRIAGE?

47 Notify/Involve Outside Authorities/StakeHolders

49 Outside Containment/Treatment Procedures

46 Evacuation of Community Necessary?

45 Evacuation of CO Plants Necessary?

YES

NO 46a

NO 45a

53 Procure Backups

53a

52 Backup Sites?

YES 52a

NO

50 2

44 Containment/ Treatment Effective?

NO

YES

51 Resume Operations?

NO

YES

55 CM Training

54 Pre/PostCrisis Audits

56 NoFault Organizational Learning

57 Improved CM Capabilities

58 Next Crisis

59 1

51

reputational crisis, we contain it by attempting to isolate it psychologically (i.e., in the minds of people), by differentiating it from the rest of the organization or a particular person.

For the second option, removal, we attempt to remove physically a crisis or its effects, for example, when we physically remove a toxic spill from a particular location. If we cannot physically remove a crisis or its effects, we should try to disperse it or its effects, reduce it, or neutralize its potency.

To Evacuate or Not to Evacuate?

If containment and treatment are not sufficient (Figure 2.9, Point 44), we should decide whether the physical evacuation of an organization's facilities or its surrounding community is necessary. Note that the term *evacuation* is not meant literally. For instance, you may be faced with having to abandon or discontinue a product or even a business unit of an organization, because the damage to a particular brand, factory, plant, or product is so severe that it must be jettisoned in order to save the rest of the organization. As with everything else, evacuation cannot be considered in isolation. Outside authorities such as the public health authorities and the police probably should be notified (Figure 2.9, Box 47), if only to coordinate the community's response and

evacuation. In some cases, the crisis may be so serious that a triage of employees and the surrounding
communities must be undertaken. Finally, if the organization is unable to contain the crisis completely
on its own, outsiders should be brought in (Box 49).

Business Resumption

Once a crisis is brought under control and its effects
have been contained or mitigated to the point that they
no longer constitute a threat to the organization or its
external stakeholders, the resumption of business is the
next step (Figure 2.9, Diamond 51). If you cannot
resume full operations at an organization's sites, are
backup sites available (Diamond 52)? If they are not
available, temporary facilities may have to be found.
You may want to resume certain operations as soon
as possible to indicate to key customers that the organization is still in business and hence is both able and
willing to serve them. Any temporary backup sites
should also provide for the maintenance and storage
of critical information, computers, and telecommunications. This includes both "hot" and "cold" storage
sites. *Hot* sites enable an almost instantaneous
switchover to backup databases, computers, and tele-
phones in the event of a shutdown. This includes securing alternative trunk or communication lines from
telephone companies. *Cold* sites, on the other hand,

refer to the regular backup of key records in protected, off-site storage facilities, without immediate access to backup equipment.

A critical factor in backing up plants, facilities, information, telecommunications, and the like is that backup operations must be considered as a whole. It is no longer sufficient to back up individual sites, work stations, facilities, or pieces of equipment, since entire systems can now fail because of the complexity and the interconnectedness of technology.

Finally, backup activities require an organization to identify those of its key customers who need to be serviced quickly or continuously and on whom the organization depends for its operations. Likewise, you should find out who the critical vendors or suppliers of goods and services are on whom the organization depends in order to serve its key customers.

CONCLUDING REMARKS

For those readers interested in seeing how Figures 2.5, 2.7, and 2.9 relate to one another and also fit into the overall process of CM, Figure 2.10 is available; it shows the entire CM process. (Readers can obtain a copy of Figure 2.10 by mailing in the card included with this book.)

By now, it should be apparent why effective CM during a crisis requires effective preparation before it occurs. Most of the key decisions and activities that must be considered and undertaken during a crisis cannot be performed effectively if you or your organization lack the proper preparation and CM capabilities. Accordingly, we turn next to the activities you should perform before and after a crisis.

Notes

1. Ian I. Mitroff and Thierry C. Pauchant, *We're So Big and Powerful Nothing Bad Can Happen to Us: An Investigation of America's Crisis-Prone Corporations* (New York: Birch Lane Press, 1990).
2. Ibid.
3. See Ian I. Mitroff and Ralph H. Kilmann, *Corporate Tragedies, Product Tampering, Sabotage, and Other Catastrophes* (New York: Praeger, 1984).
4. Mitroff and Pauchant, *We're So Big and Powerful.*
5. Thierry C. Pauchant and Ian I. Mitroff, *Transforming the Crisis Prone Organization* (San Francisco: Jossey-Bass, 1992).
6. Ibid.
7. Ibid.
8. Ibid. See also Christine M. Pearson and Ian I. Mitroff, "From Crisis Prone to Crisis Prepared: A Framework for Crisis Management," *Academy of Management Executive* 7 (1993): 48–59.

THREE

Auditing an Organization's CM Strengths and Vulnerabilities

WHAT TO DO BEFORE
AND AFTER A CRISIS

A paradox is associated with CM: We cannot understand fully what we need to do during crisis unless we first understand what we need to do and have in place before a crisis; at the same time, we cannot understand fully what we need to do beforehand unless we understand what we will be required to do during a crisis. There is no easy way out of this. The best that we can do is work back and forth between these two critical phases so that over time, executives and their organizations become better prepared.

After every crisis or near crisis, a postincident audit should be conducted (see Figure 2.9, Point 54). The purpose of such audits is to help an organization review what it did well and learn what it needs to improve on so that it will be better prepared to face its next crises (Boxes 54–57). Although such reviews are essential, many organizations do not bother with them and hence are not well prepared to face their next crisis (Box 58).

THE PRE- AND POSTCRISIS AUDIT

Figure 3.1 is an overview of the activities comprising a thorough CM audit. It does not distinguish between a precrisis and a postcrisis audit.

A Precrisis Audit

A precrisis audit typically includes interviews with the key members of an organization's corporate staff and/or the key members at a particular plant or site. The interviews should be designed to probe for four critical factors that lead an organization to be either CM prepared or CM prone. A sample set of interview questions is given in Table 3.1.

The same questions are asked of every top executive on an organization's corporate staff, so as to identify common perspectives as well as significant differences. Determining an organization's CM strengths and weaknesses is too important to be left to the judgment of a single person; all senior executives should participate in such evaluations.

In addition, you cannot find the information necessary to determine an organization's CM strengths and weaknesses solely by studying its CM manuals, documents, training programs, and so forth. Although such sources are a valuable source of infor-

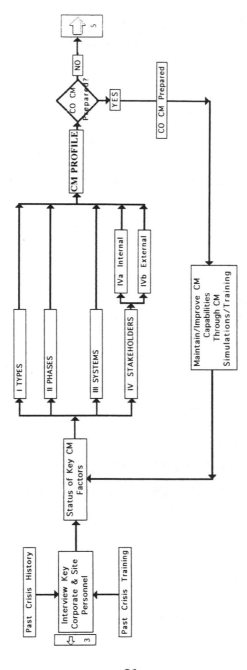

Figure 3.1. Precrisis and postcrisis audits.

61

TABLE 3.1. CRISIS MANAGEMENT AUDIT GUIDE

The following questions indicate the general kinds of issues that should be raised in an interview. These questions may also be used as a general guide to explore certain issues further.

1. What is your definition of a crisis for your organization?

2. In your opinion, what kinds of crises is your organization prepared for, and why?

3. What kinds of crises is your organization not prepared for, and why?

4. Does your organization have a crisis management team (CMT)?

   a. If your organization has a CMT, are you a member of it?

   b. Who else is on the CMT?

   c. What kind of training, if any, has your team been given?

   d. Has your team undergone conflict resolution training?

5. What kinds of early warning systems, or signal detection mechanisms (SDM), for crises does your organization have?

   a. For which crises?

   b. Are the SDMs integrated?

   c. Are they dispersed throughout your organization?

6. Is the detection of crises specifically rewarded?

7. Is probing for crises discretionary or mandatory, and is it rewarded?

   a. Do you conduct formal training sessions or simulations for crises? If so, for what kinds of crises?

   b. How frequently?

   c. What do the sessions specifically test for?

TABLE 3.1. (continued)

d. Do they probe for and uncover key, taken-for-granted assumptions?

8. Describe the kinds or ranges of damage containment mechanisms your organization has.

   a. For which kinds of crises?

   b. How frequently are they inspected or maintained?

   c. How frequently are they reviewed for design flaws?

9. Describe your organization's business recovery and/or backup systems.

   a. For which kinds of crises?

10. Does your organization have formal backup systems for computer and telecommunication systems?

    a. Does your organization have both "hot" and "cold" storage sites?

11. Does your organization conduct formal review sessions of past crises and near crises, not to blame individual people but, rather, to improve its ability to prevent and respond better to future crises?

12. Describe the state of your organization's primary technologies.

    a. Are fault-tree analyses performed in regard to probable failure modes?

    b. Are formal risk and assessments performed?

13. How do the following characteristics of your organization contribute to the prevention or cause of crises?

    a. Formal organizational structure?

    b. Job descriptions?

    c. Reward mechanisms?

    d. Formal and informal channels of communication?

    e. Authority/power structure?

(continued)

TABLE 3.1. CRISIS MANAGEMENT AUDIT GUIDE (continued)

14. Have human factor analyses been performed with regard to how operators and maintenance personnel can cause or prevent crises?

15. Describe the general culture or mind-set of your organization.

    a. What denial mechanisms or beliefs hinder effective crisis management?

    b. Does the general culture or mind-set of your organization contribute to effective CM?

16. What stakeholders are explicitly considered in the formation and execution of CM plans and procedures?

17. What are your organization's CM capabilities? What evidence do you have to back up your beliefs?

    a. How well do these capabilities match your organization's crisis plans?

18. Is CM tied into or integrated with other key programs such as

    a. Total quality management (TQM)?

    b. Environment?

    c. Health and safety?

    d. Ethics?

    e. What else?

19. Is CM part of everyone's job?

    a. Why?

    b. Why not?

mation, at some point you should talk to people to find out what CM means to them and how they view their organization's CM preparedness.

Because these interviews are such an important part of the CM audit, we recommend that they be conducted by outsiders who have been specially trained to conduct and analyze interviews. Furthermore, the interview will not yield valuable information unless strict confidentiality and anonymity are guaranteed, and insiders generally cannot provide such assurances. The interviewer must be able to reassure those being interviewed that under no circumstances will the responses of individuals be identified, that only aggregate data will be given to the organization for consideration.

We usually interview the following people in order to compile a collective portrait of an organization's CM strengths and weaknesses: (1) chief executive officer, or CEO; (2) chief financial officer, or CFO; (3) chief operating officer, or COO; as well as the most senior executive in charge of (4) security, (5) human resources, (6) health and safety, (7) environment, (8) corporate communications and public affairs, (9) government affairs, (10) public relations, (11) quality assurance, (12) head of management information systems, (13) ethics officer, (14) corporate training, and (15) head of technical operations.

The interview questions (Table 3.1) explore four factors that have been shown to play a significant role in crises: (1) types, (2) phases, (3) systems, and (4) stakeholders.[1] *Types* refers to the kinds (scope, breadth) of crises for which an organization is prepared, as well as the reasons for selecting those particular crises. *Phases* refers to how well an organization is prepared to detect, contain, recover from, and learn from crises. *Systems* refers to how well an organization is prepared to manage the complex systems that can either cause or prevent a crisis. Finally, *stakeholders* refers to the critical parties, including both individual people and institutions, who would be affected by a crisis or who could affect the organization's ability to manage a crisis.

Generally, the results of a CM audit are presented in several forms: (1) a written report that summarizes the major findings and makes recommendations for improvement, (2) an on-site oral presentation of the results, and if possible, (3) a CM profile that shows graphically an organization's CM strengths and weaknesses with regard to the preceding four factors. Figure 3.2 shows whether an organization is performing poorly, questionably, or well on each of these four factors. Because Figure 3.2 is part of the software

Figure 3.2. A CM profile showing an organization's CM strengths and weaknesses.

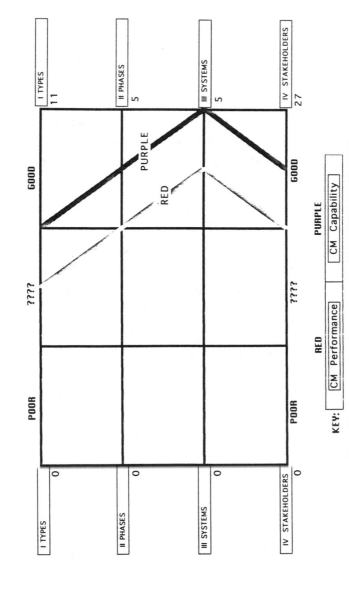

Today's Date=
Today's Time=

Date of Graph=
Time of Graph=

I TYPES 11

II PHASES 5

III SYSTEMS 5

IV STAKEHOLDERS 27

GOOD

PURPLE

RED

GOOD

????

POOR

????

POOR

I TYPES 0

II PHASES 0

III SYSTEMS 0

IV STAKEHOLDERS 0

RED | PURPLE

KEY: | CM Performance | | CM Capability |

Note: If only one color shows, then the two profiles are identical.

67

package CrMgt, we shall discuss it in more detail in Chapter 5. One of the strengths of CrMgt is that it allows the user to evaluate quantitatively the CM strengths and weaknesses of his or her organization. The software package also automatically plots a graph like the one shown in Figure 3.2.

A CM profile is one of the principal outputs of the CM audit process shown in Figure 3.1 and is indicated by the box in Figure 3.1 labeled CM PROFILE. An organization's CM strengths and weaknesses are used to determine whether or not the organization is CM prepared, as shown on the right side of Figure 3.1. If an organization is judged to be CM prepared, it is not an excuse for relaxing. Rather, the box at the bottom of Figure 3.1 is meant to indicate that an organization must continue to work hard to maintain and improve its CM capabilities through constant simulations and training.

A Postcrisis Audit

A postcrisis audit differs from a precrisis audit in several respects. First, the chief goal of the postcrisis audit is to identify lessons to be learned from a particular "trigger" event and how best to integrate those lessons into an organization's daily operations and CM practices. Second, a postcrisis audit is prompted by a particular crisis or near crisis. Third, it focuses principally on that event and only secondarily on an organization's overall crisis preparedness.

Like a precrisis audit, a postcrisis analysis concentrates on the four factors that play a significant role in virtually all crises: (1) types, (2) phases, (3) systems, and (4) stakeholders. Because of the specificity of postcrisis audits, it is difficult to construct a general audit guide, but there are important areas that should be covered:

1. What happened? Determine the basic facts (disputed and undisputed.

2. What caused the incident.

3. Which factors (internal and external to the organization) led to this type of occurrence? Did the structure, culture, technology, or people in the organization contribute to the crisis potential? Did the business environment or pressure from external stakeholders create or exacerbate the organization's vulnerability to this type of crisis?

4. When responding to the crisis, what was done well?

5. What was done poorly?

6. Does the organization continue to be vulnerable to this type of crisis?

7. Could a crisis of this type lead to other crises? What are they?

8. What steps must the organization take to reduce its risk to future crises, both this type and others?

As with precrisis audits, it is desirable to interview the broadest possible range of executives, managers, and employees with knowledge of the incident and also those affected by it. External stakeholders should be interviewed whenever possible, as the perspective of those outside the organization is often different from that of insiders and can reveal important information that might otherwise go unnoticed.

Although no two crises are the same, identifying the specific nature of a crisis and its causes is necessary in order to understand the organization's vulnerability to that general type of crisis. The contributing factors are equally important because they provide clues to structural weaknesses that may make an organization susceptible. Analyzing an organization's response is also a good way to identify the systems and stakeholders at risk from a particular type of crisis.

One of the most difficult aspects of CM is integrating the lessons learned from crises and near crises. When conducting a postcrisis audit, it is helpful to secure a commitment in advance to use the audit findings for future improvement. This requires a willingness by the organization to engage in "no-fault" learning. Although this is difficult, in our experience, it is precisely this commitment to no-fault learning that distinguishes successful postcrisis audits from pro forma exercises.

THE FOUR MAIN FACTORS OF CM

Figures 3.3 through 3.9 illustrate the kinds of issues that are associated with the four main CM factors: (1) types, (2) phases, (3) systems, and (4) stakeholders. Although we will consider each figure, we will not discuss every aspect of them at this point. (The figures are also part of the software package CrMgt, which is used to determine an organization's CM profile. For this reason, the figures ask the user to make various judgments that are scored automatically. The scores are then used to compare an organization's performance during a crisis with its preparation or capabilities before the crisis.)

Types

Since both the numbers and the different forms that each crisis assumes are unlimited, no organization, even with the best of resources, can plan for every possibility. Furthermore, no crisis ever happens exactly as expected. Therefore, CM plans should not be considered as ends in themselves; instead, they should be considered part of the process of thinking about and training for the "unthinkable."

Figures 3.3 and 3.4 show eleven basic types of crises as well as examples of the various possible subtypes. It is important to understand that we are not claiming that these, and only these, eleven exhaust all possible kinds of crises. Instead, Figures 3.3 and 3.4 identify, to the best of our current knowledge, the variety of possible crises. We have found from previous research that crises fit into eleven groups or families, those listed in Figures 3.3 and 3.4.[2] Our research has also shown that the "best," or CM-prepared, organizations do not prepare for just one kind of crisis. Instead, they prepare for a variety of crises; in effect, they compile a *crisis portfolio*, by preparing for at least one type of crisis in each of the eleven categories. They also do not get sidetracked over precisely which subtype they should prepare for. Rather, they understand that even though they are not identical, the different subtypes in a particular category are similar. In addition, because no crisis ever happens exactly as expected, it does not matter

Figure 3.3. The eleven types of crises and their subtypes.

MAIN TYPES	SUBTYPES	CURRENT CRISIS ANY of the SUBTYPES?	AT LEAST ONE SUBTYPE in CM PLANS?
1. Criminal Attacks	1. Copycats 2. Employee Violence 3. Product Tampering 4. Sabotage 5. Sexual Harassment 6. Terrorism 7.	☒ YES ☐ NO ☐ DON'T KNOW	☒ YES ☐ NO ☐ DON'T KNOW
2. Economic Attacks	1. Boycotts 2. Hostile Takeovers 3. Stock Devaluation 4. Strikes 5. 6. 7.	☒ YES ☐ NO ☐ DON'T KNOW	☒ YES ☐ NO ☐ DON'T KNOW
3. Loss of Proprietary Information	1. False Rumors 2. Copyright Infringement 3. Counterfeiting 4. Proprietary Information 5. 6. 7.	☐ YES ☒ NO ☐ DON'T KNOW	☐ YES ☒ NO ☐ DON'T KNOW
4. Industrial Disasters	1. Major Contaminations 2. Major Explosions 3. Major Fires 4. Major Releases 5. Major Spills 6. 7.	☒ YES ☐ NO ☐ DON'T KNOW	☐ YES ☒ NO ☐ DON'T KNOW
5. Natural Disasters	1. Blizzards 2. Earthquakes 3. Electrical Storms 4. Floods 5. Tornadoes 6. Typhoons	☒ YES ☐ NO ☐ DON'T KNOW	☐ YES ☒ NO ☐ DON'T KNOW
6. Breaks in Equipment & Plants	1. Computer Breakdowns 2. Distribution Net Defects 3. Major Operator Errors 4. Major Product Defects 5. Major Product Recalls 6. Manuf/Plant Defects 7. Security Breakdowns 8. Telecommunications Breaks 9. Quality Defects 10.	☒ YES ☐ NO ☐ DON'T KNOW	☒ YES ☐ NO ☐ DON'T KNOW

Total CM Performance
Score = 4
0-Poor.....11-Excellent

Total CM Plan
Score = 7
0-Poor.....11-Excellent

MAIN TYPES		SUBTYPES	CURRENT CRISIS ANY of the SUBTYPES?	AT LEAST ONE SUBTYPE in CM PLANS?
7	Legal	1. Major Corporate Lawsuits 2. Major ClassAction Suits 3. Major Distributor Suits 4. Major Officer Liabilities 5. Major Product Liabilities 6. 7.	☒ YES ☐ NO ☐ DON'T KNOW	☒ YES ☐ NO ☐ DON'T KNOW
8	Reputational Perceptual	1. Damaging/False Rumors 2. Damage to Reputation 3. Projection onto Brand/Logo 4. 5. 6. 7.	☒ YES ☐ NO ☐ DON'T KNOW	☒ YES ☐ NO ☐ DON'T KNOW
9	Human Resources Occupational	1. Employee Violence 2. Executive Succession 3. Family Violence 4. Faulty Corporate Culture 5. Sexual Harassment 6. 7.	☒ YES ☐ NO ☐ DON'T KNOW	☒ YES ☐ NO ☐ DON'T KNOW
10	Health	1. AIDS 2. Environmental Contamination 3. JobRelated Injuries 4. JobRelated Deaths 5. 6.	☒ YES ☐ NO ☐ DON'T KNOW	☒ YES ☐ NO ☐ DON'T KNOW
11	Regulatory	1. Adverse CO Regulations 2. Adverse Special Interests 3. Adverse Industry Regulations 4. 5. 6.	☒ YES ☐ NO ☐ DON'T KNOW	☐ YES ☒ NO ☐ DON'T KNOW

-Total CM Performance
Score- 4

0=Poor.....+11=Excellent

Total CM Plan
Score- 7

0=Poor.....+11=Excellent

74

which subtype within a particular cluster is considered. What counts is that an organization has prepared for the possibility of at least one type occurring within each cluster.

Crisis-prepared organizations also prepare for at least one subtype in each of the main categories, because each type of crisis may be either the cause or the effect of another kind of crisis. For example, an economic downturn may set off a wave of criminal activities that in turn may make an industrial disaster more likely. Once again, it is important to take a systems point of view with regard to effective CM preparation. Like total quality management (TQM), CM is a systemic process. It does no good to prepare for only one type of crisis if another type can equally threaten or harm the organization.

CM-prepared organizations go even further. For instance, all organizations, not merely food and pharmaceutical companies, are subject to product tampering. The French publisher Larousse experienced a crisis that illustrates this point: As avid consumers of wild mushrooms, the French use the Larousse encyclopedia to differentiate between poisonous and edible mushrooms. On two pages, side by side, are pictures of mushrooms that are safe to

Figure 3.4. The eleven types of crises and their subtypes, continued.

eat opposite those that are not. For some unknown reason, the labels of the two pictures were reversed. Whether this was done by a careless editor or was an intentional, criminal act is not known and perhaps never will be.

The point is that every organization faces the possibility of some form of product tampering. For this reason, an integral part of the CM training and preparation process is brainstorming by the top members of an organization to consider how every category or type of crisis can apply to their organization. In order to come up with a broad spectrum of realistic examples, the members need to be prodded to think generally, not literally.

Phases

Figure 3.5 shows the five components of the factor *phases*: (1) signal detection, (2) preparation/prevention/probing, (3) damage containment, (4) business recovery, and (5) learning.

The first phase, *signal detection*, is the monitoring and heeding of early warning signals that point to the possible occurrence of a crisis. The explosion of the space shuttle *Challenger* is a prime example

Figure 3.5. The five components of the phases factor.

PHASES

	Org Performed Well on the Factor in the Current Crisis?	Org Has CM CAPABILITY for the Particular Factor?
Signal Detection		
1. SD Criteria Formulated		
2. Barriers to SD Identified		
3. Barriers to SD Removed		
4. SD Mechanisms Integrated	☐ YES ☒ NO ☐ Don't Know	☒ YES ☐ NO ☐ Don't Know
5. SD Rewarded for Diverse Crises		
6. SD Rewarded Throughout Org		
7. SD Integrated w/Key Programs		
Probing (Detection)		
1. Mandatory Inspection Key Eqpmt		
2. Mandatory/Constant Training	☐ YES ☒ NO ☐ Don't Know	☒ YES ☐ NO ☐ Don't Know
3. Freq Discussions between Designers and Operators		
4. Freq Discuss between Operators and Maintenance		
5. Reporting Bad News Rewarded		
Damage Containment		
1. DCs for Wide Range of Crises		
2. DCs Constantly Inspected/Maint		
3. DCs Constantly Tested	☒ YES ☐ NO ☐ Don't Know	☒ YES ☐ NO ☐ Don't Know
4. DCs Constantly Upgraded		
5. DCs Constantly Improved		
6. Crisis Command Center		
7.		
Business Recovery		
1. Backup Manufact Sites		
2. Backup Telecommunications		
3. Backup Computers	☒ YES ☐ NO ☐ Don't Know	☒ YES ☐ NO ☐ Don't Know
4. Hot/Cold Information Storage		
5. Backup Mgt Sites		
6. Crisis Command Center		
7.		
No-Fault Learning		
1. Critique of Key Assumptions		
2. Mandatory Review Past Crises		
3. Reporting Bad News Rewarded		
4. Mandatory Review Key Lessons	☒ YES ☐ NO ☐ Don't Know	☐ YES ☒ NO ☐ Don't Know
5. Acknowledge Anniversaries		
6. Allow Sharing of Emotions		
7. Action Plans for Improvement		

"YES"= Org Did/Does Have a Particular Belief or Property

Give an OVERALL Rating for Each Factor

CM Performance Score = 3   0=Poor.....5=Excellent   CM Capability Score = 4

77

of a crisis whose early warning signals were ignored. The Report of the President's Commission on the Space Shuttle Accident uncovered a comprehensive trail of memos before the event clearly explaining that the O-ring was improperly designed and hence could cause a catastrophic failure of the shuttle.

The difficulty, of course, is that organizations are bombarded with signals of all kinds. However, it has been found that organizations that are crisis prepared make a point of constantly probing and scrutinizing their operations and management structure for warnings of potential crises. In other words, they do not leave the detection of important signals to chance. Instead, they put in place mechanisms to increase the chances of early detection.

The second phase, preparation/prevention/probing, is doing as much as possible to avoid crises and to prepare better for those that still manage to occur. This phase does not imply that all crises can be prevented; instead, it emphasizes that the adage "if it ain't broke, don't fix it" has no place in CM.

Those organizations that can be classified as crisis prone exhibit a very different "mind-set" from those that can be classified as crisis prepared. As in the case of signal detection, preparation/prevention/probing in crisis-prepared organizations is the careful and constant probing of operations and management structures for potential "breaks and cracks" before they become too big to "fix." An example of a lack of attention to preparation/prevention/probing is Union Carbide's chemical explosion in its Bhopal, India, plant, during which thousands of people died because they had not previously been made aware of a basic safety response (i.e., covering one's nose and mouth with rags to avoid ingesting methyl isocyanate gas).

Damage containment is intended to keep a crisis from spreading to other, uncontaminated parts of an organization or its environment. A tragic example is the environmental costs of the Exxon Valdez oil spill, which were intensified by both poor damage containment mechanisms, such as inefficient oil-skimming equipment, and ineffectual damage containment activities, as well as the time lost in communicating among divisions of Exxon. A critical point regarding damage containment mechanisms and activities is that they are virtually impossible to invent during a crisis. Rather, effective CM requires the continued development and testing of CM capabilities before a crisis. In short, effective CM is proactive, not reactive.

During the recovery phase, crisis-prepared organizations implement short-term and long-term business recovery programs to facilitate the resumption of normal business operations. Programs designed for this purpose include the identification of minimal services and procedures needed to resume business, the reassignment of people to new jobs, and the designation of alternative operating sites.

The last phase, learning, is the reflection on and examination of the lessons that have been learned from the organization's own crisis experiences, as well as those of other organizations. Many organizations gloss over this phase because of the mistaken belief that an examination of the past will "only re-open old wounds." But almost exactly the opposite has been found to be true. Following a crisis or near disaster, crisis-prepared organizations examine and compare the factors that enabled them to perform well with those that impeded their CM performance, without assigning blame. By contrast, crisis-prone organizations emphasize finding blame instead of learning lessons.

A valid CM audit assesses how well an organization is performing on each of these phases. (The scoring system used is a relatively simple one. Every yes that an organization gives to a particular component adds a one to its score. In comparison, the scoring system for the preceding variable types is much more complicated and is explained in Chapter 5.)

Figure 3.6 is based on Figure 3.5. It asks managers to evaluate in detail the damage containment strat-

Figure 3.6. Damage containment strategies for each type of crisis.

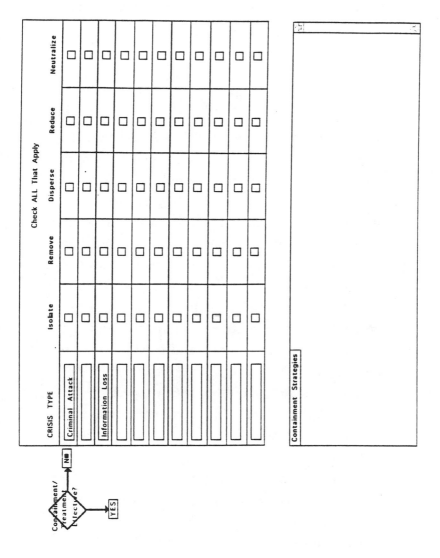

Check ALL That Apply

CRISIS TYPE	Isolate	Remove	Disperse	Reduce	Neutralize
Criminal Attack	☐	☐	☐	☐	☐
	☐	☐	☐	☐	☐
Information Loss	☐	☐	☐	☐	☐
	☐	☐	☐	☐	☐
	☐	☐	☐	☐	☐
	☐	☐	☐	☐	☐
	☐	☐	☐	☐	☐
	☐	☐	☐	☐	☐
	☐	☐	☐	☐	☐
	☐	☐	☐	☐	☐
	☐	☐	☐	☐	☐

Containment/
Treatment
Effective?

YES

No

Containment Strategies

81

egies for each type of crisis their organization faces. (Figure 3.6 also is part of the software package contained in the program CrMgt.)

Systems

Studies of a wide range of crises reveal that they occur because of breakdowns in the linkages among organizations, people, and technologies. No assessment of risk can be accurate unless it looks systematically at the interactions of all three subsystems. Unless an organization analyzes how (1) individual human operators and managers interact with technological systems, (2) people's limitations affect their reactions under stressful conditions, and (3) organizational factors (such as reward systems and communications channels) affect individual human responses, risk assessments will be incomplete at best.

CM plans and procedures need to specify the crisis roles and activities, lines of communication, membership on CM teams, backup resources, facilities, and schedules that people and systems in the organization must assume during a crisis. Just as important as documented plans and procedures is the effect of an organization's informal culture on its formal plans and procedures. One of the distinguishing hallmarks of crisis-prone organizations is a faulty mind-set or belief structure. A study conducted by the University of Southern California Center for Crisis Management repeatedly found the same rationalizations that organizations used to explain why they thought they did not need to take CM seriously:[3] "We're big enough to handle any crisis"; "Accidents are just the cost of doing business"; "CM is a luxury that we can't afford"; "If we have a major crisis, then someone else will rescue us." This study found that crisis-prone organizations subscribe to these beliefs seven times more than do crisis-prepared organizations.

Figure 3.7 is similar to Figure 3.5, except that each of the detailed attributes in each of the boxes has a negative connotation. Thus a "yes" response means that an organization does not have a particular defect. Also, to make the scoring easier and hence to reduce the amount of time spent going through the figures, the reader is asked merely to estimate an overall rating for each factor as a whole.

Stakeholders

Many parties are affected by and affect crises. *Stakeholders*—individual persons, special-interest groups, and institutions that affect or are affected by a specific organization—represent the diversity of views an organization should consider when formu-

SYSTEMIC FACTORS

	Org Performed Well on the Factor in the Current Crisis?	Org Has CM CAPABILITY for the Particular Factor?

Org / Infrastructure

1. Breakdown of Authority
2. Breakdown in Communication
3. Breakdown of CMT
4. Breakdown of Controls
5. Breakdown of Rewards
6. Breakdown of Reporting
7.

☒ YES ☐ NO ☐ Don't Know ☒ YES ☐ NO ☐ Don't Know

Factors

1. Operator Errors
2. Faulty Maintenance
3. Faulty Man-Machine Design
4. Faulty Man-Org Interface
5. Faulty Systems Controls
6. Poor Training
7.

☒ YES ☐ NO ☐ Don't Know ☒ YES ☐ NO ☐ Don't Know

Technology

1. Age of Equipment/Plants
2. Design Flaws
3. Faulty Maintainance
4. Severe Operating Conditions
5. Severe Operating History
6.
7.

☒ YES ☐ NO ☐ Don't Know ☒ YES ☐ NO ☐ Don't Know

Org / Culture

1. Belief Can Handle Anything
2. Belief CM Not Worth the Money
3. Belief Org Is Invulnernable
4. Denial of Need for CM
5. Denial of Magnitude of Threats
6. Denial of Possibility of Threats

☒ YES ☐ NO ☐ Don't Know ☒ YES ☐ NO ☐ Don't Know

Beliefs of TopMgt

1. Belief Can Handle Anything
2. Belief CM Not Worth the Money
3. Belief They Are Invulnernable
4. Denial of the Need for CM
5. Denial of Magnitude of Threats
6. Denial of Possibility of Threats

☐ YES ☒ NO ☐ Don't Know ☒ YES ☐ NO ☐ Don't Know

"YES" = Org Performed Well by NOT Having the Particular Defect

"YES" = Org Has CM Capability by NOT Having the Particular Defect

Give an OVERALL Rating for Each Factor

CM Performance   Score = 4   0=Poor.....5=Excellent   CM Capability   Score = 5 lating its CM plans and procedures. The current trend in management is to expand the number of relevant stakeholders beyond employees, managers, and unions to include customers and vendors. Effective CM requires an even greater expansion of relevant stakeholders to include parties even further removed from the organization, such as special-interest groups, local politicians, and even competitors. In sum, crisis-prepared organizations monitor and factor into their CM plans a much wider range of stakeholders than do crisis-prone organizations. For any organization, a systematic examination of diverse stakeholders and their associated properties is a critical part of the CM process. Figures 3.8 and 3.9 indicate the kinds of considerations that are necessary in the CM process with regard to major stakeholders, both internal and external. The questions on internal stakeholders focus on CMT membership, training, and access information.

DEVELOPING CM CAPABILITIES

The purpose of a CM audit is to identify an organization's major strengths and weaknesses so that a clear plan of action can be developed and imple-

Figure 3.7. The systemic factors of a crisis.

INTERNAL STAKEHOLDERS

Officers	Positive Role in Current Crisis?	CMT Training?	Member of CMT?	LOCATION	TELEPHONE #
CEO	☒ YES ☐ NO	☒ YES ☐ NO	☒ YES ☐ NO		Dial 213-555-1212
COO	☐ YES ☒ NO	☒ YES ☐ NO	☒ YES ☐ NO		Dial 213-555-1212
CFO	☐ YES ☒ NO	☒ YES ☐ NO	☒ YES ☐ NO		Dial 213-555-1212
Legal	☐ YES ☒ NO	☒ YES ☐ NO	☒ YES ☐ NO		Dial 213-555-1212
Security	☐ YES ☒ NO	☒ YES ☐ NO	☒ YES ☒ NO		Dial 213-555-1212
PA	☐ YES ☒ NO	☒ YES ☐ NO	☒ YES ☐ NO		Dial 213-555-1212
HR	☒ YES ☐ NO	☒ YES ☐ NO	☒ YES ☐ NO		Dial 213-555-1212
Engineering Health	☒ YES ☐ NO	☒ YES ☐ NO	☒ YES ☐ NO		Dial 213-555-1212
Environment	☒ YES ☐ NO	☒ YES ☐ NO	☐ YES ☒ NO		Dial 213-555-1212

Crisis Performance Score = 4
CM Capability Score = 9
0 Poor.....9 Excellent

mented to enhance its CM capabilities. Without such capabilities, an organization will find it very difficult to carry out the decisions and actions demanded in a crisis.

Figures 3.10 and 3.11 outline the main ingredients of a process intended to develop an organization's CM capabilities. The figures are essentially two different versions of the same thing. Both are intended to help an organization become CM prepared.

One of the first steps in developing an organization's CM capabilities is forming and training a CMT. The members of the CMT need to be selected with care and caution, and new members should not be added indiscriminately. A general rule is that a team should contain the smallest number of persons necessary to cope with a crisis. Most organizations' CMT has representatives from at least the following divisions: (1) Legal, (2) Security, (3) Human Resources, (4) Health and Safety, (5) Quality Assurance or Operations, and (6) Corporate Communications or Public Affairs. The organization's CEO should not automatically be made the leader of the CMT, although by the very definition of a crisis, the CEO and the top executives naturally need to have full information about the crisis and some degree of involvement.

Figure 3.8. CM considerations regarding internal stakeholders.

EXTERNAL STAKEHOLDERS

STAKEHOLDER	Positive Role in Current Crisis?	PreCrisis Relationship?	Positive History?	CONTACT	TELEPHONE #
FBI	⊠ YES □ NO	□ YES ⊠ NO	⊠ YES □ NO		Dial 213-555-1212
State Police	⊠ YES □ NO	□ YES ⊠ NO	⊠ YES □ NO		Dial 213-555-1212
Local Police	⊠ YES □ NO	□ YES ⊠ NO	⊠ YES □ NO		Dial 213-555-1212
FDA	⊠ YES □ NO	□ YES ⊠ NO	⊠ YES □ NO		Dial 213-555-1212
State Health	⊠ YES □ NO	⊠ YES □ NO	⊠ YES □ NO		Dial 213-555-1212
Local Health	⊠ YES □ NO	□ YES ⊠ NO	⊠ YES □ NO		Dial 213-555-1212
EPA State	⊠ YES □ NO	□ YES ⊠ NO	⊠ YES □ NO		Dial 213-555-1212
Environmental Local	⊠ YES □ NO	□ YES ⊠ NO	□ YES ⊠ NO		Dial 213-555-1212
Environmental	⊠ YES □ NO	□ YES ⊠ NO	□ YES ⊠ NO		Dial 213-555-1212

Crisis Performance Score = 14   0=Poor.....18=Excellent

CM Capability Score = 11

One of the most important roles of a CMT is that of a *facilitator*. The main functions of the facilitator are to make sure that all the team members have access to the same body of information and that no single point of view dominates the discussion.

THE ROLE OF SIMULATIONS IN CM

Simulations and training exercises are an essential part of the development of every organization's CM capabilities. A good simulation tests every aspect of the CM process described in this and the preceding chapter, including as many as possible of the dynamics represented in Figures 2.5, 2.7, and 2.9. (For instance, the types of crises represented in a simulation should test an organization's ability to respond simultaneously to multiple crises.) This means that the simulation should not be so transparent that the decisions and actions to be taken at every step are obvious or reduced to a single choice. Rather, a good simulation contains generous amounts of uncertainty. This forces the members of the CMT to state their assumptions as clearly as they can, reach agreement where they can, tolerate disagreement where they cannot, and identify at each step what they (1) know,

---

Figure 3.9. CM considerations regarding external stakeholders.

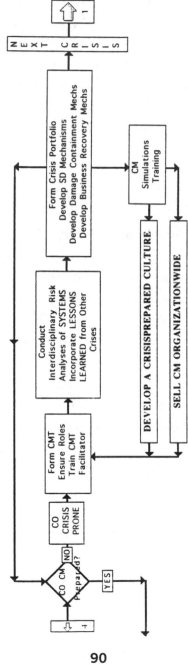

Figure 3.10. Development of CM capabilities.

(2) do not know, (3) must do immediately, (4) must postpone, and (5) must monitor and keep track of over time. The CMT also needs to keep track of both the details and the big picture of CM. An example of a simulation that we have constructed and used with organizations is given in Table 3.2.

As with all the various aspects of CM, we cannot emphasize too strongly that everything pertaining to an organization's CM capabilities and preparation should be tailored to its unique needs and circumstances. In CM, there are no useful "off-the-shelf" tools and procedures, and any person or group pretending to offer such aids should be rejected immediately.

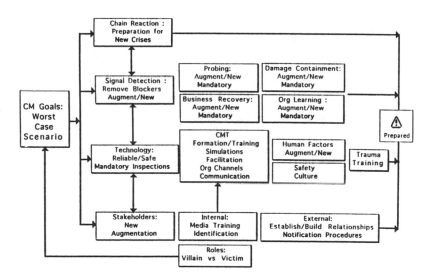

Figure 3.11. Development of CM capabilities, continued.

TABLE 3.2. HYPOTHETICAL CMT TABLETOP EXERCISE

Segment 1
MONDAY, 7:26 A.M.

As the Today Show fades to the local weather report, you catch just the tail end of Susan Jones's words: "This only substantiates the concerns we've expressed. We can't afford any more mishaps like Saturday's crisis at ChemCo's plant. I promise the fight is not over. As your attorney general, it is my duty to protect the people of this state."

Segment 2
MONDAY, 8:50 A.M.

Approximately thirty-six hours ago you should have received the first call regarding the serious fire and explosion at one of ChemCo's main plants, and now you may be facing the potential destruction of Blooming Gardens and the surrounding farmlands. There is also the possibility that a stretch of the Blue River could be contaminated by spills entering the sewers adjacent to the chemical plant. You can't help but think that something should have been done to prevent this disaster. Maybe if the incident had occurred when the superintendent was on duty, the damages could have been minimized.

Segment 3
MONDAY, 11:00 A.M.

An official from the state's Department of Natural Resources has phoned to inform you that they will be investigating any connection to ChemCo regarding the residents' complaints: Dead trout have been reported floating in the Blue River and Green Bay, with evidence of contamination by ChemCo.

Segment 4
MONDAY, 12:00 NOON

A status update confirms your worst suspicions. Toxic material leaking into drains has infiltrated the sewer system,

TABLE 3.2. (continued)

washing into the waste treatment plant. Projections indicate that all the flora and fauna of the treatment process may be killed by the leakage. How could the inspection conducted earlier this year have missed this problem? The engineers assure you that even though there were clear indications that pressure was building, measurements remained within established tolerance limits. Looking back, it all seems so obvious. If only a veteran operator had been taking the sample on Saturday. Surely someone who knew the system as well as his or her own car would have discovered the building pressure. Surely someone more experienced could have foreseen these problems.

Segment 5
MONDAY, 1:00 P.M.

A full picture of what is happening is beginning to emerge:
- 8:47 P.M., Saturday: The incident is first reported.
- 9:00 P.M., Saturday: Plant emergency response members are notified and go to the scene of the incident.
- 11:00 P.M., Saturday: The twenty-one injured people are taken to a hospital. The CMT is notified that four are confirmed dead and eight of the injured remain hospitalized.

Segment 6
MONDAY, 3:00 P.M.

CNN begins with a brief interview with a long-standing friend of ChemCo, Professor Frank Smith from Blossom State University. You're relieved that ChemCo is now getting some positive press, as Smith tells the interviewer, "ChemCo works to protect people and the environment as part of everything they do." You hope his statement may take some of the heat off your company. That makes two on your list of allies: The

(continued)

TABLE 3.2. HYPOTHETICAL CMT TABLETOP EXERCISE
(continued)

local union issued a statement earlier this morning assuring its members that it would continue to support ChemCo.

Two on your list of allies. And how many adversaries? Citizens for Environmental Advocacy has joined local environmentalist groups to express concern about the plant and the industry. You've had calls from competitors, with offers of assistance as well as criticisms of your presumed lack of attention to the facility. Some of ChemCo's national trade association representatives will be flying to the site later today. But your biggest surprise has been the media. Although the stories have certainly not been slanted in ChemCo's favor, the reporters have been willing to abide by your guidelines, and they have covered your briefings in a straightforward manner. If you could only convince them that ChemCo's intentions were earnest, that this site was a good and safe workplace.

Segment 7
MONDAY, 5:00 P.M.

Although there is some comfort that the site emergency response team performed well, you are concerned and angry that the area CMT was not notified more quickly. In addition, your thoughts are jolted once again. Your legal adviser reports that rumors of class-action suits are beginning to circulate.

Note: A group works on each time segment for approximately thirty minutes or less.

An Example

A recent crisis audit of a power utility that we performed illustrates its importance, especially in regard to what it can reveal about an organization. With regard to *types*, the audit clearly showed that in line with its business and mission, the utility was prepared mainly for natural disasters, especially those that would interrupt electrical service to its customers. Thus the organization had in place not only plans to deal with such disasters but also a day-to-day operational capability of responding to electrical and ice storms, fires, tornadoes, and other natural disasters. The utility was also rather well prepared for any threats to its equipment (the failure of electrical transformers) and technical systems in general.

In short, the utility was generally well prepared for technical crises, but it was not well prepared for large-scale systems accidents. For instance, it would not be prepared if five of its plants, located throughout its territory of operation, went out simultaneously. Most troubling, the audit revealed that the utility was not prepared for a broad range of human-induced crises such as sabotage or the kidnapping of an executive. It was certainly not prepared if a human crisis like sabotage led to a severe, large-scale technical crisis such as the shutdown of the entire system. This deficit was made even worse by the fact that in general, security was lax at key locations.

The organization was especially deficient with regard to *phases*. For instance, not only were its signal detection mechanisms few and far between, but the audit disclosed that one of the most important sources of early warning signals was blocked rather effectively by the organization. It seems that maintenance personnel were in the best position to discover potential trouble spots. At the end of each shift, they filled out an evaluation form indicating the status of the machinery that they had inspected and/or on which they had performed maintenance. In theory, these forms were reviewed by their shift supervisors and passed on to their superiors. The trouble was that the status of the maintenance personnel was the lowest of any in the organization, and for this reason, their reports were generally ignored.

Notice that the low status of maintenance personnel affects not only the CM variable signal detection but systems and stakeholders as well. That is, the effects are systemic. The low status of the maintenance personnel compromises the detection of early warning signals and could also affect the safe operation of key equipment. In addition, this discovery also demonstrates the importance of analyzing the impact of a wide variety of stakeholders on an organization's crisis potential.

CONCLUDING REMARKS

Chapters 1, 2, and 3 introduced both the big picture and the details of CM, and they also covered what you need to consider and do before and after a crisis.

We believe that every organization should perform a crisis audit before it experiences a crisis. We also recommend that every organization perform at least one crisis audit a year and also after the occurrence of a crisis. Such audits are for the purpose of learning what patterns, if any, can be detected in an organization's responses, and they are invaluable in identifying crisis preparation strengths and weaknesses.

Notes

1. Thierry C. Pauchant and Ian I. Mitroff, *Transforming the Crisis Prone Organization* (San Francisco: Jossey-Bass, 1992). See also Ian I. Mitroff and Christine M. Pearson, *Crisis Management: A Diagnostic Guide for Improving Your Organization's Crisis Preparedness* (San Francisco: Jossey-Bass, 1993).

2. Ibid.

3. See Pauchant and Mitroff, *Transforming the Crisis Prone Organization*; see also Mitroff and Pearson, *Crisis Management*.

FOUR

The Systemic
Nature of CM

MORE EXTENSIVE TRAINING
AND PREPARATION FOR CM

The preceding chapters discussed the importance of conducting pre- and post-CM audits and also many of the issues associated with developing an organization's capabilities to manage a crisis. In this chapter, we will continue discussing capabilities, especially training exercises and procedures.

RESPONSIBILITIES AND ROLES

In Chapter 3, we talked briefly about the role of a CMT's facilitator. Here we shall consider the responsibilities and roles of the other members of a CMT (Figure 4.1).

The primary role of a legal counsel on a CMT is not to veto particular actions or declarations. Rather, a legal counsel is present mainly to advise a CMT of the legal ramifications of its decisions and actions. A

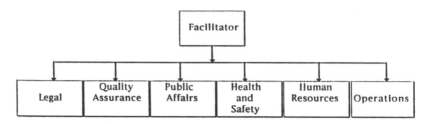

Figure 4.1. The CMT's roles and responsibilities.

legal counsel thus needs to be an integral part of a problem-detecting and problem-solving team. Thus, if the CMT as a whole decides to engage in an action that has serious legal ramifications, the legal counsel can recommend how the actions can be carried out with as little harm as possible. This is critical in those cases where the legal counsel disagrees with the CMT's actions.

Likewise, security's role is not merely to point out serious threats and potential breaches to an organization's security. It is on the team to suggest how such breaches might be controlled and to provide a technical perspective regarding the impacts of specific security procedures on the organization. This is especially important in the case of criminal activities in which security procedures that are too tight or severe can be viewed as punitive and hence encourage the very things they are designed to prevent. As many organizations have discovered too late, strict security programs can alienate internal stakeholders, for example, employees, to such a degree that they may provoke violent responses. The principal question is how security can be designed with the cooperation of employees. We know of organizations in the food industry that have received cooperation from their labor unions in designing procedures to identify potential tamperers and saboteurs. In these cases, the union cooperated because the resultant losses of company products could threaten jobs.

The role of quality assurance (QA) is critical to the food and pharmaceutical industries. QA and Operations often play an invaluable role in averting potential crises. For instance, in food jars, crystallized sugar can look like pieces of glass. QA can help diagnose potential crises and defuse them with proper information to consumers. For example, claims of food poisoning and specific types of food sicknesses can often be defused. A case in point is hepatitis A, which requires an incubation period before the disease appears and can be properly diagnosed. Thus if a customer contends before the incubation period is over, that he or she developed the disease, that claim is false. QA also can join security to identify tampering efforts.

One of the most important roles of a CMT is that of health and safety. Ideally, every organization should have maps and inventories of each of its sites showing the location of potentially hazardous and toxic chemicals, products, and the like. It should also have a complete listing of Haz Mat procedures plus detailed training in their proper use in order to handle any major spill or release.

Public affairs (PA) and corporate communications (CC) are the main communications liaisons with the media and other important external stakeholders, but they must train all the members of a CMT in how to respond to the media. PA and CC thus need to be integral members of the CMT, since they cannot be effective communicators unless they are familiar with the potential causes of various types of crises and the actions that the organization has taken to prevent or to contain them. PA and CC cannot function in a vacuum.

SYSTEMS THINKING

Most discussions of CM miss one of the CMT's most important functions: *critical systems thinking.*[1] There is no better way to illustrate such thinking than with two crises that took place at two important organizations, Sears and NASA.

A few years ago, Sears faced a financial crisis because its auto-repair stores were not bringing in enough revenue. Thus the initial crisis was financial, and how Sears responded shows why that no action should be taken until the causes of the crisis have been determined and the effects on the organization of various responses can be gauged.

Sears undertook a series of actions designed to bring more cash into its stores, based on the following idea: Why not offer a bonus plan to our Auto Repair employees for bringing in extra business? Sears hoped that by this means it could reverse its negative cash flow.

The bonus plan worked, but not in the ways intended: Sears Auto Repair employees brought in more money by recommending unnecessary repairs to consumers. When news of this broke, Sears faced a worse crisis than the original one, by inadvertently damaging its corporate image as a company that its customers could trust. This loss of trust threatened to reduce Sears's financial revenues even more, thus exacerbating the very crisis that prompted the bonus plan in the first place.

What went wrong? Sears failed to consider the effect of the bonus plan on the whole organization. Such a plan would have worked only if Sears had fostered the kind of culture that produced trust in both its customers and its employees. No action ever takes place in a vacuum; instead, every action affects and, in turn, is affected by its key stakeholders.

Consider another example. NASA was faced with an unacceptable level of defects in some of its main programs. In an attempt to decrease the number of defects, it also introduced a bonus plan, in this case, to find defects. But this incentive also triggered an unanticipated negative response: A number of employees deliberately created defects so that they could identify them and collect the bonus!

Such examples can be multiplied ad nauseam. For instance, Honda executives were recently accused of demanding kickbacks from high-volume dealers in order to boost their fixed salaries. Because a profitable dealer could expect to make considerably more money than the corporate executives could, some executives demanded payoffs before they would ship cars to dealers. The problem was not only in the pay or reward system but also in the values of some parts of the Honda culture. Even a bad pay system does not justify blackmail.

No action, no matter how desirable it seems on the surface, should be undertaken until its potential positive and negative effects on the entire system have been determined.

AN EXAMPLE OF A SYSTEMIC MESS-UP

The following case shows the importance of a systemic approach to CM. Many of the organizations with which we work are leaders in their fields. The subject of this case—we will call it Beta Group—is no exception. In addition to being a world leader in its field, Beta Group, like many companies in many industries today, is finding that its external relationships are becoming increasingly complex. Customers are vendors; competitors are partners; and partners are customers—sometimes all at once! Beta Group's crisis was caused by a failure to manage effectively this complex relationship. The incident caused severe embarrassment to the organization's CEO, jeopardized millions of dollars of current business, and threatened a thirty-year relationship with a customer/partner/competitor, not the sort of thing we expect to happen to leading-edge organizations.

Three incidents—a casual telephone remark from one CEO to another, the decision not to continue an existing partnership on an upcoming project, and the failure to anticipate the severity of the customer/partner/competitor's reaction—coalesced to create a serious relationship crisis between the two organizations, which jeopardized Beta Group's reputation with other customers and external stakeholders.

Two types of factors contributed to the crisis. The first was organizational, the structure and culture of Beta Group and the nature of its business. The second set of factors arose from the nature of the crisis management (CM) process itself. Organizations that are unfamiliar with CM are especially susceptible to difficulties related to this second set of factors.

Beta Group's culture is intensely rational, an "engineering" mentality, and this rational/analytic worldview is combined with a strong emphasis on agreeableness. The organization's structure is highly decentralized and entrepreneurial, with a factory-driven business focus, and its success in recent years is attributed to this structure. Conversely, the potential weaknesses that this structure has created are the suboptimization of financial performance at the business unit level, an emphasis on the product rather than on the customer, an arrogance regarding technical competency, and the fragmentation of strategic objectives.

Some of the characteristics of Beta Group's industry also were important factors influencing the crisis. Like most large organizations, Beta Group has a diversified product line serving a broad array of customers. Most of its business is conducted in fairly stable environments, in which long-term relationships are a hallmark of success. Some of Beta Group's business, however, is conducted in a highly competitive environment characterized by high-risk, high-stakes business deals; fluid relationships; and deal-to-deal partnering. This is the area in which the precipitating events occurred.

The structure of Beta Group and the nature of its business combined to create competing objectives.

Peculiar to this crisis was the tension between the objective to maximize business unit performance and the objective to maximize account relationships. When one of Beta Group's divisions decided to discontinue a partnership with an organization—call it Z Company—that decision was not seen as creating a potential risk, even though Z Company was also a thirty-year customer. Because it did not have a crisis management program, Beta Group had no means of monitoring early warning signals of potential crisis and no way to evaluate systematically the possible risks.

To make matters worse, because of Beta Group's decentralized structure and entrepreneurial operating style, there was no reason to tell Beta's CEO about this decision. Then, when Beta Group's CEO was talking to Z Company's CEO about a separate project, Beta's CEO made a remark about working with Z Company on other, similar projects, which was interpreted by Z Company's CEO as reversing the decision made at the business unit level. At Beta Group, however, there was (1) no knowledge of the business unit decision at that time and (2) no intent to reverse the decision. In fact, when the "perception" of Z Company was brought to the attention of senior executives at Beta, the original decision to discontinue the partnership was reexamined. Beta finally decided that Z Company would understand the reasons for the decision and accept it.

But this was not what happened. In fact, Z Company's response was far worse than Beta Group could have imagined. The CEO of Z Company felt betrayed, and he ordered an immediate discontinuation of all business relations with Beta Group. For several months he refused all attempts of reconciliation. The discontinuation of business with Beta Group affected several of its business units and divisions, threatening millions of dollars of revenue. In addition, Z Company had sister companies that also had substantial relationships with Beta Group. For a time, it was feared that the wrath of Z Company's CEO could jeopardize those relationships as well. Finally, almost six months later, the two CEOs met. After several more meetings and a concerted effort by the executive management of Beta Group, most business relations have been restored.

This crisis illustrates just how serious the consequences can be when people fail to communicate clearly and accurately. Our analysis of the events indicates that there was no intention by Beta Group to misrepresent or mislead its longtime friend and ally. Yet that was exactly the perception of Z Company's CEO, and the consequences for the relationship between the two organizations could have been disastrous.

On closer inspection, it is clear that Beta Group's strengths with regard to conducting normal business do not serve to contain, and may actually contribute to, crises. Many of these factors, both individually and collectively, reinforce the fragmented nature of Beta Group's organization: Individual business units are rewarded for maximizing their own special interests without regard to the effects on the organization as a whole. Thus the breach in relations between Beta Group and Z Company was due more to structural and cultural factors than to individual actions.

DEVELOPING A CRISIS AWARENESS

In order to prevent a crisis, an organization must determine what exactly it would be. One way of "developing a crisis awareness"—after conducting a CM audit—is as follows: Assemble the executives who will form the core of the organization's CMT, or whose endorsement is critical if the organization is to go forward. All executives are asked to write down examples of what they believe would constitute a crisis for their organization, whether or not anyone else agrees with them. External and/or internal group facilitators then ask each executive in turn to read one example from the list. Each is written on a flip chart so that all can see them. No disagreement is allowed at this point, so that the process will not be shut off or slowed down. The only discussion permitted is that necessary to allow others to understand what a particular person means by his or her definition of a crisis. Also, each person is asked to give only one example so that every member can participate without one or more persons hogging the floor.

The exercise is repeated for as many rounds as necessary until the group is satisfied that it has included the various kinds of crises that they think could happen to their organization. The group is then asked to write down on another piece of paper both the crises from the first list, of those that it feels its organization is prepared to handle, and those that it feels it is not. Once again the executives are asked to give only one example per turn. When the group feels that it has responded as well as it can, the next part of the exercise is introduced.

The executives are asked to write down what they feel their organization would do well and do poorly during a crisis. As before, the responses are tabulated for all to see.

Finally, the group is split into two or three subgroups, each of which is asked to choose a crisis for which their organization is not currently well prepared. Each group is then asked to create a variety of scenarios that would cause additional crises as a result of the first one. They then should pick one of these additional crises to examine in greater detail. For the crisis they select, they are asked to describe a worse-case, but plausible, situation in which the crisis could take place. They also are asked to think about early warning signals that could be monitored for signs of a potential crisis and to specify the damage containment mechanisms that should be in place before the crisis occurs. They also should identify those aspects of their organization's current culture that will work for and against it in handling the crisis. Last, they should write down those steps that they can take immediately in their part of the organization in order to lower its crisis potential. Above all, they are encouraged to think systemically. As a group, what can they do to prepare and protect their organization as a whole?

THE ASSASSIN-TEAM EXERCISE

Other exercises probe even deeper. Since they contain elements of the Sears and NASA examples just described, they must be undertaken with caution, for unless the organization already has a positive culture, these exercises can backfire.

Anywhere from twelve to twenty people at most are brought together and are split into three or four subgroups. They are given the following instructions: Each of you knows more about your organization than any of the authors or facilitators every could. Each of you is to become a member of an assassin team. Using your detailed, inside knowledge of your organization, think of the most creative ways to destroy the organization without getting caught, or to delay being caught for as long as possible. In addition, make whatever you come up with as hard as possible to discover. Some of the teams are asked to work solely from an inside perspective (e.g., an internal fraud scheme); others are asked to work solely from the outside (e.g., in cahoots with external stakeholders); and still others are asked to work on both the inside and the outside simultaneously.

When the teams have completed this part of the exercise, they share their schemes, but no critique is permitted at this point. The only questions allowed are those necessary to understand a team's reasoning.

After the schemes are presented, the counterassassin teams are formed. Each new team is asked to think of ways to foil the plots of the assassin teams. In this way, the group as a whole can test and discover for itself what is feasible and what is not. Needless to say, this exercise requires extreme trust, as otherwise it can give dangerous ideas to dangerous people.

SELLING CM

There is no single aspect connected with CM that is not systemic or does not have a systemic side to it. The selling of CM to an organization is an important case in point. The development of an organization's CM capabilities typically starts with one or a few champions. Because they have "seen the light," they cannot understand why others do not immediately see the urgency of improving their organization's CM capabilities.

Rarely, however, is a single champion successful in selling CM to an organization unless, of course, he or she is in a powerful position. Instead, this person must embark on a generally slow and tortuous process of educating and selling CM to the multitude of internal and external stakeholders. As a result, successful and unsuccessful strategies are quickly distinguished.

Selling CM and building a culture committed to CM is a good example of systems thinking in action. Because a lone champion may not be sufficient to sell CM to an organization, he or she must find a wide range of allies, that is, sell CM to his or her counterparts throughout the organization. But internal allies are not enough. In addition, the champion and his or her allies must win the support of their counterparts at other organizations in their industry and their industry trade associations. In this way, the message is reinforced from several sources.

Even this is usually not enough. Most organizations must undergo repeated crises before the message finally gets through that effective CM requires constant precrisis preparation. And even the occurrence of multiple crises is rarely sufficient. Unless there is an underlying infrastructure and a commitment to CM, once a crisis has passed, the organization usually retreats to its "hear no evil, see no evil" posture.

CONCLUDING REMARKS

One organization with which we have worked exhibits nearly all the features covered in this chapter. This organization has adapted to its particular circumstances each of the CM processes and procedures described in this book, and each of its major plants and divisions has a CMT.

In addition, a version of Figure 2.10, which shows the relationship of Figures 2.5, 2.7, and 2.9 to one another (the reader can obtain a copy of Figure 2.10 by mailing in the order card included with the book), has been prepared for every conceivable crisis, indicating the special problems that each would create. In addition, each member of a CMT has a customized version of Figure 2.10 that shows his or her roles and responsibilities in regard to a particular crisis. In order to ensure that these roles and responsibilities will be coordinated, each CMT has a facilitator to integrate individual views. Finally, since the organization is a multinational corporation, crisis programs and procedures have been prepared for each of its regions around the world.

In order to be effective, CM must be rooted firmly in systems thinking. CM is systemic because crises not only affect a system as a whole but also result from the breakdown of systems as a whole. For this reason, CM must be integrated into an organization's existing systemic programs, such as total quality management, environmentalism, and health and safety, which cut across functions, departments, and business units. It also is important to recognize that there are natural and considerable overlaps and synergies among systemic programs. Such overlaps must be encouraged, especially in this age of downsizing, in which no program has all the resources it requires. Today's—and tomorrow's— organizations must be designed or operated using systemic approaches.[2]

Notes

1. See Ian I. Mitroff and Harold Linstone, *The Unbounded Mind* (New York: Oxford University Press, 1993); see also Russell L. Ackoff, *The Democratic Corporation, a Radical Prescription Recreating Corporate America and Rediscovering Success* (New York: Oxford University Press, 1994).

2. See Ian I. Mitroff, Richard O. Mason, and Christine M. Pearson, *Framebreak: The Radical Redesign of American Business* (San Francisco: Jossey-Bass, 1994).

FIVE

CrMgt

SOFTWARE FOR CM

This chapter describes the software that accompanies this book. We believe that technology is important, even though we recognize that unless it is managed effectively, technology may help contribute to the occurrence of crises. This observation does not mean, however, that technology should never be used; rather, it is a warning that it should be used appropriately.

CRMGT: A SUPERCARD STAND-ALONE SOFTWARE PROGRAM

The software you need to run is included on the disk accompanying this book. If you have a Macintosh computer, you do not need any additional software to run the program. But if you have an IBM PC, you will need to buy a software package from the

Allegiant Corporation that will allow you to run SuperCard programs on a PC.

The program runs best if your computer is one of the latest Macs, that is, a Power Mac. In addition, the program was expressly written for a Mac computer screen seventeen inches or larger. Although you can still run the program if your computer screen is smaller than seventeen inches, you will have to do a lot of "scrolling around." In addition, the "big picture" will also be much harder to see.

Place the disk in the hard drive of your personal computer. The program CrMgt on the disk was written in an application software system labeled SuperCard, a registered trademark of the Allegiant Corporation. The particular software version you have is a *stand-alone application.* This means that you do not need to know, or concern yourself directly with, the SuperCard programming language or system because all the programming has been done for you. The term *stand-alone* means precisely that.

First, load the program CrMgt from the disk onto your hard disk. Then double click on the icon CrMgt to start the program. When you first open the program, you should see something like Figure 5.1. Actually, you should see something more than what is shown in Figure 5.1, but ignore this for the time being. Figure 5.1 is a close relative of Figure 2.1. In

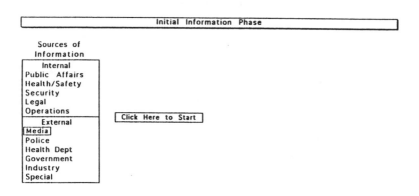

Crisis Management:
A Decision CheckList
© Ian I Mitroff, 1994

Figure 5.1. The first step of the CrMgt program (the first part of Figure 5.5).

fact, Figure 5.1 turns into Figure 2.1 with the first step of the program. To start the program, click your mouse once on the rectangle in Figure 5.1 labeled "Click Here to Start." You then should see Figure 5.2.

Before proceeding further, we need to say a little bit about how SuperCard works. When you clicked your mouse on the rectangle "Click Here to Start" in Figure 5.1, you actually executed a small software program contained in the rectangle. In the language of SuperCard, you clicked the mouse on the *button* "Click Here to Start."

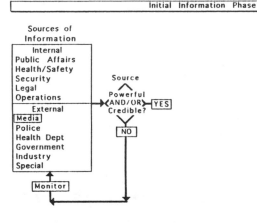

Figure 5.2. The second step.

SuperCard belongs to the class of programming languages known as *object oriented*, which means that you must do certain things like click a button or move your mouse into a certain region (*field*) in order for the program to proceed.

The "card" in SuperCard refers to the fact that SuperCard programs like CrMgt are essentially an organized series of screens stacked like a series of cards in a file cabinet. Each screen contains a certain number of buttons, text fields in which you can write, or graphic illustrations. You can do or file only so much on a particular screen before it becomes over-loaded. SuperCard allows you to create as many screens as you like (within, of course, the limit of your computer's memory) to accomplish a particular task.

The screens in CrMgt have been organized so that the CM processes described in Chapters 2 and 3 can be broken down into natural segments or pieces. For example, Figure 5.5 constitutes one screen of the Super-Card program CrMgt. Figures 5.1, 5.2, 5.3, and 5.4

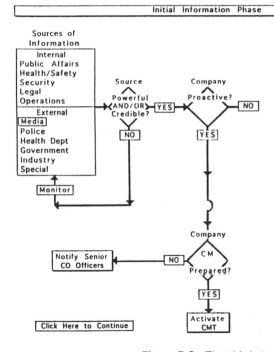

Figure 5.3. The third step.

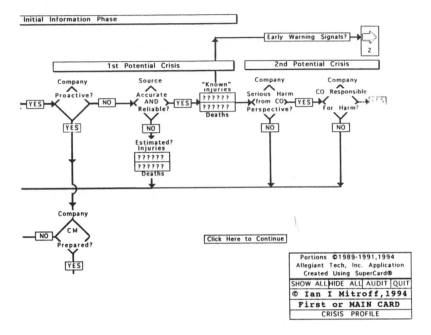

Figure 5.4. The fourth step.

allow you to see Figure 5.5 in stages. Recall from Chapters 2 and 3 that we presented many of the figures in stages so that they would not be as overwhelming as they would if you saw them all at once. The computer program CrMgt is also organized in this fashion to make the figures as "user friendly" as possible.

Figure 5.5 contains a number of features with

Figure 5.5. The first, or main control, card (Figures 5.1, 5.2, 5.3, and 5.4).

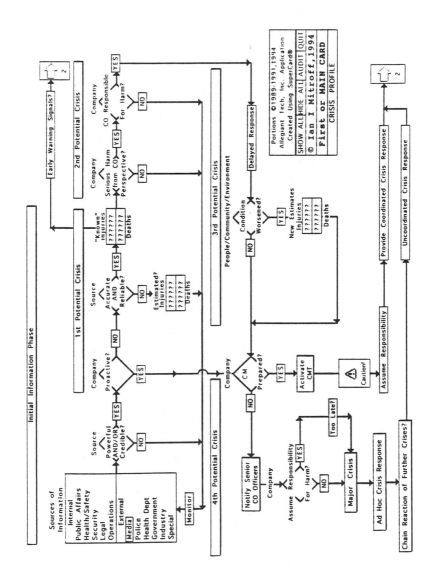

First or MAIN CARD
CRISIS PROFILE

127

which you should become familiar. First, Figure 5.5 is the first, or main control, card. You always start and end the program with this card even if you decide to quit the program from another card or screen. Second, when the program starts, you should always see Figure 5.1 and also the trademark and copyright material in the lower right-hand corner of Figure 5.5. If you click your mouse on the rectangular button labeled "Show All," you will automatically bypass Figures 5.2, 5.3, and 5.4 to go directly to Figure 5.5. At any time, if you wish to examine parts of Figure 5.5, you can begin the process again by clicking the mouse on the button "Hide All," and you will automatically return to Figure 5.1.

Figure 5.5 contains a number of other important features as well. If you have a color monitor, you will see that the various buttons are in different colors, to call attention to those parts of a complex process that we wish to emphasize. Thus in the program CrMgt, the color red usually stands for a potential crisis point, and green usually stands for a CM strength.

If you move your mouse into the sets of text fields with question marks, you can enter the numbers of estimated or known injuries and deaths or the actual or expected dollar amounts lost in a particular crisis. The program CrMgt has been designed to be used as a working guide before, during, and after a crisis.

After you have finished working with Figure 5.5, you can go to the other screens in a number of ways. You can click the mouse on Button 1 on Figure 5.5. The button will automatically transfer you to Card 2. Or if you wish to proceed directly to a precrisis or postcrisis audit, you can click the mouse on the button "AUDIT" in the lower right-hand corner of Figure 5.5. If you wish to quit the program, simply click the mouse on the button labeled "QUIT." Just before the program shuts down, you will see the screen briefly return to Figure 5.1. In this way, the program will automatically start from the initial condition shown in Figure 5.1.

If you decide to proceed to Card 2, you should see Figure 5.6. Like Figure 5.5, the second card also

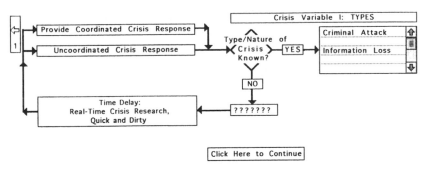

Figure 5.6. The second card.

unfolds in stages so that you can use the program with a minimum of distraction from the inherent complexity of the CM process. This feature also allows you to proceed at your own speed.

You have a number of options available in Figure 5.6. First, if you click the mouse in the diamond labeled "Type/Nature of Crisis Known?" you will go to a much later card in CrMgt, showing the range of different kinds of subcrises. We strongly urge you not to do this at this point, but if you do, click on the "Return" button in order to get back to Figure 5.6.

If you click on the "YES" button to the immediate right of the diamond in Figure 5.6, you should see Figure 5.7. You can then click on all the various *types* of crises that you believe are part of the particular crisis you are facing. That is, a crisis can contain one or all of the choices shown in Figure 5.7. You make your choices by moving the mouse into each of the checkmark boxes to the immediate left of each crisis type. Figure 5.7 shows the case in which the particular crisis you are confronting is a combination of (1) Criminal Attack, (2) the Loss of Proprietary Information, and (3) an attack on the Perception/Reputation of an organization.

If you want to change your choices at any time, click on the buttons representing other crises or the button "Clear All." Clear All resets all the buttons; that is, it removes the checkmarks from each box.

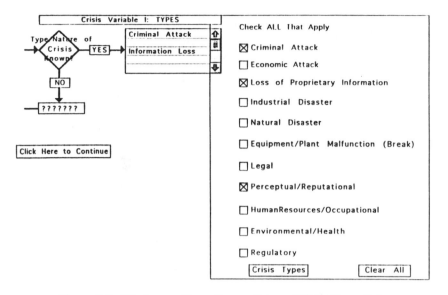

Figure 5.7. What you will see if you click on YES in Figure 5.6.

In Figure 5.6, if you click on the "NO" just below the diamond labeled "Type/Nature of Crisis Known?" you should see Figure 5.8. In this figure, you cannot click on any of the different types of crises, since based on your response (no), you indicated that you do not know the exact type of the current crisis that you are facing. Thus, by clicking NO, all the checkmarks are erased, and the text field to the immediate right of the YES button to the immediate right of the diamond is "wiped clean" or erased of crisis types.

Figures 5.6 and 5.7 list all the crises you checked off as part of the overall crisis you were facing. Crimi-

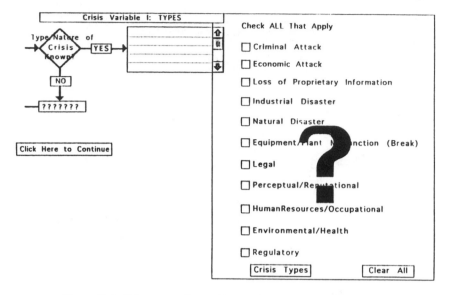

Figure 5.8. What you will see if you click on NO in Figure 5.6.

nal Attacks and Information Loss are shown in the small text field to the immediate left of the big box containing the eleven basic types of crises. The small text field is known as a *scrolling field*, which allows you to store a lot of information in a small space. By scrolling up or down, you can see all the information contained in the field. To do this, click the mouse in one of the small vertical arrows in either direction. If you click in the down direction, you should see that Perceptual/Reputational is included there as well. In other words, the computer automatically places each crisis type on a separate line. Thus, Crisis 8, Perceptual/Reputational, is placed in Line 8 in the small scroll field.

From Figure 5.7, by clicking on the box "Crises Types," it is possible to go to another card (which we describe later) that gives a complete listing of the subtypes of the eleven basic types of crises. We strongly urge you not to do this at this time. We mention this feature at this point only because once you become familiar with the program, you will want to jump around to take advantage of its features.

When you have finished with Figures 5.7 and 5.8, click on "Click Here to Continue." You should then see Figure 5.9. You also could have reached Figure 5.9 from Figure 5.6 if you had clicked on the "Con-

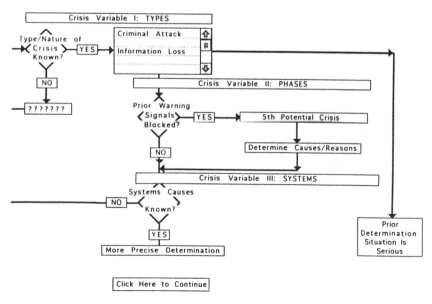

Figure 5.9. Part of what you will see if you click on "Click Here to Continue."

tinue" button there. In Figure 5.9 if you click on the YES button immediately below the diamond labeled "Systems Causes Known?" you will be transferred to a later card that allows you to specify what you believe are the systems causes of the current crisis you are facing. Again, we urge you not to do this at this time. But if you do, click "Return" to get back to Figure 5.9.

If you click on "Click Here to Continue," you will finally see Figure 5.10. As in Figure 5.5, you can always return to Figure 5.6 by clicking on "HIDE." Or you can always get to Figure 5.10 by clicking on "SHOW" as soon as you get to Figure 5.6. Or you can go immediately to the crisis audit by clicking on "AUDIT," and so on, for each of the various features.

At any time, if you feel you know more about the type of crisis you are facing, you can always reach Figure 5.7 by clicking on the YES button to the immediate right of the diamond labeled "Type/Nature of Crisis Known?" in figure 5.6.

To continue to the third card, click the mouse on Button 3 at the bottom of Figure 5.10. The upper part of Figure 5.11 will then appear. Since this card does not contain as many details as the others do, the full figure is displayed at once. If you click the mouse in

Figure 5.10. A complete view of Figure 5.9.

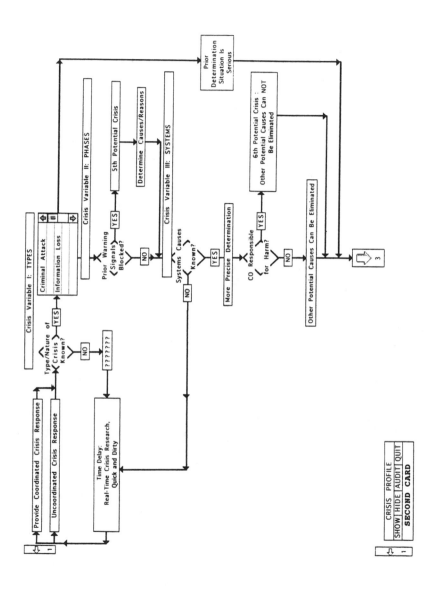

135

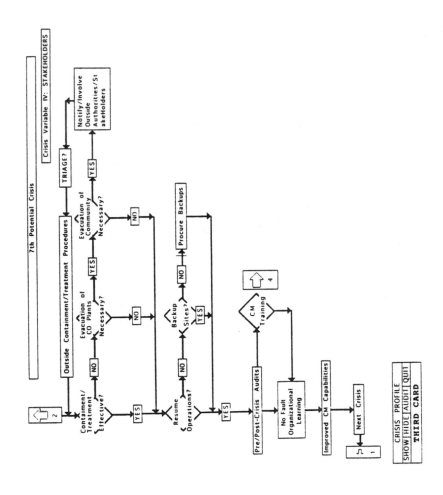

7th Potential Crisis

Crisis Variable IV: STAKEHOLDERS

136

| Has ANYTHING Changed? | | **DAMAGE CONTAINMENT STRATEGIES** | | | | | |

Figure 5.12. Part of what you will see if you click on Diamond 44 in Figure 5.11.

the middle of the Diamond "Containment/Treatment Effective?" in Figure 5.11, you will see Figures 5.12 and 5.13. Whenever you first click the Diamond, you will always see the box in the extreme upper-left-hand corner of Figure 5.12. If the types of crises from Figure 5.7 have not changed, click the mouse on the NO button in Figure 5.12 to continue. By clicking NO, you also will not change the damage containment

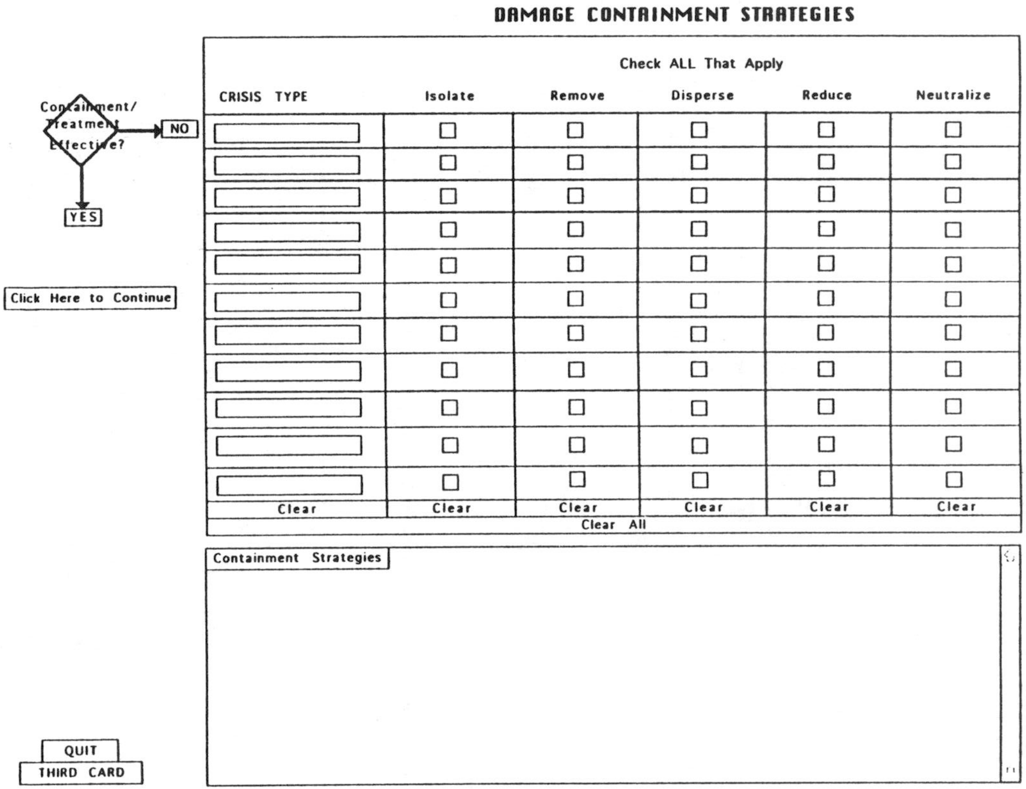

Figure 5.11. The third card.

options in Figure 5.13. If, on the other hand, you have changed your assessments of the types involved in the particular crisis you and your organization are facing, then all the checkmarks pertaining to the damage containment options in Figure 5.13 will be reset to the blank position. If at any time you wish to change your responses, you can also click on the various "Clear" buttons near the middle of Figure 5.13.

Figure 5.13 is in effect a worksheet, as are all the cards or screens in CrMgt. They allow you to try out and examine various strategies, options, and so on. Figure 5.13 also has a text field at the bottom that allows you to enter any notes you wish to record. To return to Figure 5.11, click on the "Click Here to Continue" button.

Figure 5.11 represents the "during" part of CM. To return to the first or main card from Figure 5.11, click on Button 1. You can also begin the CM audit process from Figure 5.11, by clicking the mouse on the AUDIT button at the bottom or Button 4 in Figure 5.11.

Clicking on AUDIT takes you to Figure 5.14, from which you can reach Figures 5.15 through 5.21. For instance, to reach Figure 5.15, click on "I Types"

Figure 5.13. More of what you will see if you click on Diamond 44 in Figure 5.11.

The PRE and POST-CRISIS AUDIT PROCESS

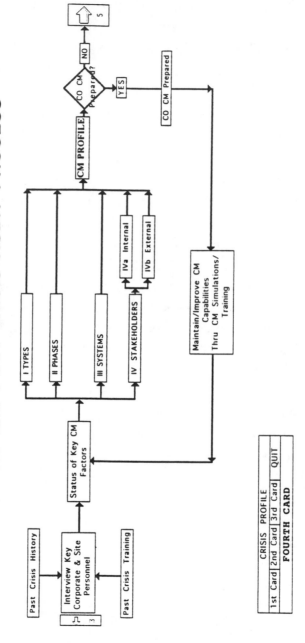

Figure 5.14. What you will see if you click on AUDIT in Figure 5.11.

140

MAIN TYPES | SUB-TYPES | CURRENT CRISIS ANY of the SUB-TYPES? | AT LEAST ONE SUB-TYPE in CM PLANS?

1 Criminal Attacks
1. Copycats
2. Employee Violence
3. Product Tampering
4. Sabotage
5. Sexual Harassment
6. Terrorism
7.
CURRENT CRISIS: ⊠ YES ☐ NO ☐ DON'T KNOW
AT LEAST ONE: ⊠ YES ☐ NO ☐ DON'T KNOW

2 Economic Attacks
1. Boycotts
2. Hostile Takeovers
3. Stock Devaluation
4. Strikes
5.
6.
7.
CURRENT CRISIS: ⊠ YES ☐ NO ☐ DON'T KNOW
AT LEAST ONE: ⊠ YES ☐ NO ☐ DON'T KNOW

3 Loss of Proprietary Information
1. False Rumors
2. Copyright Infringement
3. Counterfeiting
4. Proprietary Information
5.
6.
7.
CURRENT CRISIS: ☐ YES ⊠ NO ☐ DON'T KNOW
AT LEAST ONE: ☐ YES ☐ NO ☐ DON'T KNOW

4 Industrial Disasters
1. Major Contaminations
2. Major Explosions
3. Major Fires
4. Major Releases
5. Major Spills
6.
7.
CURRENT CRISIS: ⊠ YES ☐ NO ☐ DON'T KNOW
AT LEAST ONE: ☐ YES ⊠ NO ☐ DON'T KNOW

5 Natural Disasters
1. Blizzards
2. Earthquakes
3. Electrical Storms
4. Floods
5. Tornadoes
6. Typhoons
7.
CURRENT CRISIS: ⊠ YES ☐ NO ☐ DON'T KNOW
AT LEAST ONE: ☐ YES ⊠ NO ☐ DON'T KNOW

6 Breaks in Equipment & Plants
1. Computer Breakdowns
2. Distribution Net Defects
3. Major Operator Errors
4. Major Product Defects
5. Major Product Recalls
6. Manuf/Plant Defects
7. Security Breakdowns
8. Telecommunications Breaks
9. Quality Defects
10
CURRENT CRISIS: ⊠ YES ☐ NO ☐ DON'T KNOW
AT LEAST ONE: ⊠ YES ☐ NO ☐ DON'T KNOW

Total CM Performance Score = 4
0=Poor.....+11=Excellent

Total CM Plan Score = 7
0=Poor.....+11=Excellent

Return | PHASES | III SYSTEMS | IV STAKEHOLDERS | Types 7-11

Figure 5.15. What you will see if you click on I Types in Figure 5.14.

in Figure 5.14. From Figure 5.15, you can reach Figure 5.16 by clicking on the button "Types 7–11" at the bottom of Figure 5.15. From Figure 5.16, you can return to Figure 5.14 by clicking on "Types 1–6." You can also get to the other main crisis factors—phases, systems, and stakeholders—by clicking the buttons at the bottom of Figures 5.15 and 5.16. To return to Figure 5.14, merely click the Return button.

Recall from our discussion of Figure 5.6 that if you clicked on the diamond labeled "Type/Nature of the Crisis Known?" you were sent to a later card. That card was Figure 5.15. Thus, the Return button takes you back to the particular card from which you reached Figure 5.15.

SCORING TYPES

The scoring of your crisis preparations or plans with respect to types is easy. The total score for the CM Plan is merely the number of YES buttons checked in Figures 5.15 and 5.16, that is, the third column from the right edge of both figures. Thus the highest score you can receive under the CM Plan is 11. This is the condition in which your organization has planned for at least one crisis in each of the eleven basic types.

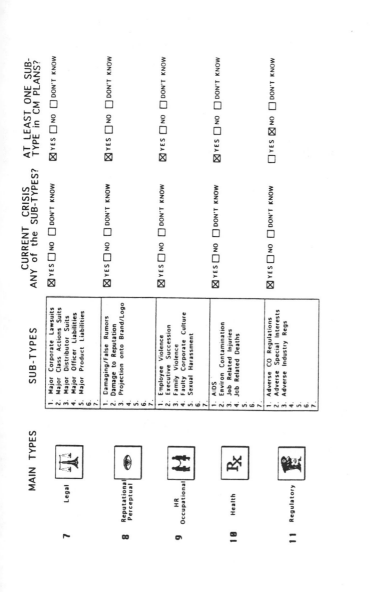

Figure 5.16. What you will see if you click on Types 7–11 in Figure 5.15.

The scoring for the Total CM Performance is more complicated because it depends on the pattern of scores for the CM Plan. For instance, consider the following example: Before a crisis an organization was prepared for crisis types 1 through 5, and so there would be a checkmark in the YES or third column from the right of Figure 5.15 for crisis types 1 through 5. The actual crisis the organization is experiencing is made up of types 1 through 5. Thus there would be a checkmark in the YES or sixth column from the right of Figure 5.15. In this case, there would be a perfect match between the crisis (or crises) the organization experienced and those for which it was prepared. In this case, we would set the Total CM Performance Score equal to the Total CM Plan Score or, in this case, 5. But suppose in addition that the crisis that the organization is experiencing is also made up of types 7 through 11. Then the YES boxes, or buttons, in the sixth column from the right of Figure 5.15 would be checked as well. But suppose too that the organization was not prepared for crisis types 7 through 11. Then the NO buttons in the second column from the right of Figure 5.15 would also be checked for types 7 through 11. In this case, we would have to lower the Total CM Performance Score to take account of the fact that the organization experienced crises for which it was not prepared.

The scoring system for the Total CM Performance Score is thus built around the fact that the total number of experienced crises is equal to the sum of the total number of matched crises and the total number of mismatched crises (i.e., those crises that the organization experienced and for which it was not prepared, as reflected in its plans). Thus, if S_1 = the total number of *experienced* crises, S_2 = the total number of *matched* crises, and S_3 = the total number of *mismatched* crises, then $S_1 = S_2 + S_3$ (A "Don't Know" response is counted as a NO.)

There are only four cases to consider. First, if $S_3 = 0$; that is, there are no mismatches, we set the Total CM Performance Score equal to the Total CM Plan Score. The three remaining cases refer to situations in which S_3 does not equal 0; that is, there are mismatches.

Second, if $S_2 = S_3$; that is, the number of matches equals the number of mismatches, we set the Total CM Performance Score equal to $S_3/3$. That is, we lower the Total CM Performance Score. In other words, the Total CM Performance Score is lowered, or penalized.

Third, if $S_2 > S_3$, we set the Total CM Performance Score equal to $S_2 - S_3$, and the Total Performance Score is lowered once again.

Finally, fourth, if $S_3 > S_2$, we set the Total CM Performance Score equal to $S_2/3$. That is, in every case, we lower or penalize the Total CM Performance Score if an organization is facing a crisis type for which it is not prepared.

PHASES, SYSTEMS, AND STAKEHOLDER SCORING

Phases, systems, and stakeholders can be reached from Figure 5.14 by clicking on the appropriate buttons. For instance, to get to Figure 5.17, click on the button "II PHASES" in Figure 5.14.

The scoring for phases, systems, and stakeholders is essentially the same. For instance, in Figure 5.18 the scores for CM Performance and CM Capability are given by the number of YES buttons that have been checked. Notice also that you can reach each of the other four main crisis factors types, phases, systems, and stakeholders from each card merely by clicking on the appropriate button at the bottom of each card.

Although they are not included in the scoring at the bottom of Figures 5.19 and 5.20, Figure 5.21 indicates that for flexibility, you can include additional names and/or roles of members of your CMT.

Figure 5.17. What you will see if you click on II PHASES in Figure 5.14.

PHASES

	Org Performed Well on the Factor in the Current Crisis?	Org Has CM CAPABILITY for the Particular Factor?
Signal Detection		
1. SD Criteria Formulated		
2. Barriers to SD Identified		
3. Barriers to SD Removed		
4. SD Mechanisms Integrated		
5. SD Mechs for Diverse Crises		
6. SD Rewarded Throughout Org	☐ YES ☒ NO ☐ Don't Know	☒ YES ☐ NO ☐ Don't Know
7. SD Integrated w/Key Programs		
Probing Detection		
1. Mandatory Inspection Key Eqpmt		
2. Mandatory/Constant Training		
3. Freq Discuss bet Designers&Ops	☐ YES ☒ NO ☐ Don't Know	☒ YES ☐ NO ☐ Don't Know
4. Freq Discuss bet Ops&Maint		
5. Reporting Bad News Rewarded		
6.		
Damage Containment		
1. DCs for Wide Range of Crises		
2. DCs Constantly Inspected/Maint		
3. DCs Constantly Tested	☒ YES ☐ NO ☐ Don't Know	☒ YES ☐ NO ☐ Don't Know
4. DCs Constantly Upgraded		
5. DCs Constantly Improved		
6. Crisis Command Center		
7.		
Business Recovery		
1. Backup Manufact Sites		
2. Backup Telecommunications		
3. Backup Computers	☒ YES ☐ NO ☐ Don't Know	☒ YES ☐ NO ☐ Don't Know
4. Hot/Cold Infor Storage Sites		
5. Backup Mgt Sites		
6. Crisis Command Center		
7.		
No-Fault Learning		
1. Critique of Key Assumptions		
2. Mandatory Review Past Crises		
3. Reporting Bad News Rewarded	☒ YES ☐ NO ☐ Don't Know	☐ YES ☒ NO ☐ Don't Know
4. Mandatory Review Key Lessons		
5. Acknowledge Anniversaries		
6. Allow Sharing of Emotions		
7. Action Plans for Improvement		

"YES" = Org Did/Does Have a Particular Belief or Property

Give an OVERALL Rating for Each Factor

CM Performance		CM Capability
Score = 3	0=Poor.....5=Excellent	Score = 4

Return | I TYPES | II SYSTEMS | III STAKEHOLDERS

147

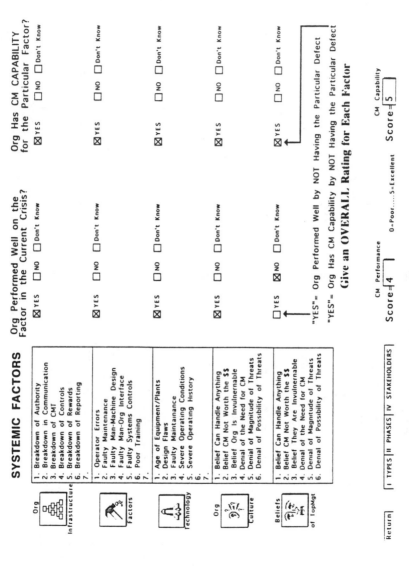

Figure 5.18. Scores for CM Performance and CM Capability.

148

INTERNAL STAKEHOLDERS

Officers	Positive Role in Current Crisis?	CMT Training?	Member of CMT?	LOCATION	TELEPHONE #
CEO	⊠ YES ☐ NO	⊠ YES ☐ NO	⊠ YES ☐ NO		Dial 213-555-1212
COO	☐ YES ⊠ NO	⊠ YES ☐ NO	⊠ YES ☐ NO		Dial 213-555-1212
CFO	☐ YES ⊠ NO	⊠ YES ☐ NO	⊠ YES ☐ NO		Dial 213-555-1212
Legal	☐ YES ⊠ NO	⊠ YES ☐ NO	⊠ YES ☐ NO		Dial 213-555-1212
Security	☐ YES ⊠ NO	⊠ YES ☐ NO	⊠ YES ⊠ NO		Dial 213-555-1212
PA	☐ YES ⊠ NO	⊠ YES ☐ NO	⊠ YES ☐ NO		Dial 213-555-1212
HR	⊠ YES ☐ NO	⊠ YES ☐ NO	⊠ YES ☐ NO		Dial 213-555-1212
Engineering	⊠ YES ☐ NO	⊠ YES ☐ NO	⊠ YES ☐ NO		Dial 213-555-1212
Health Environment	⊠ YES ☐ NO	⊠ YES ☐ NO	☐ YES ⊠ NO		Dial 213-555-1212

Crisis Performance Score | 4   CM Capability Score | 9   0=Poor......9=Excellent

| TYPES | PHASES | SYSTEMS |

| External | More Internal |

| Return | Environment |

Figure 5.19. Scores for internal stakeholders.

149

EXTERNAL STAKEHOLDERS I

STAKEHOLDER	Positive Role in Current Crisis?	Pre-Crisis Relationship?	Positive History?	CONTACT	TELEPHONE #
FBI	☒ YES ☐ NO	☐ YES ☒ NO	☒ YES ☐ NO		Dial 213-555-1212
State Police	☒ YES ☐ NO	☐ YES ☒ NO	☒ YES ☐ NO		Dial 213-555-1212
Local Police	☒ YES ☐ NO	☐ YES ☒ NO	☒ YES ☐ NO		Dial 213-555-1212
FDA	☒ YES ☐ NO	☐ YES ☒ NO	☒ YES ☐ NO		Dial 213-555-1212
State Health	☒ YES ☐ NO	☒ YES ☐ NO	☒ YES ☐ NO		Dial 213-555-1212
Local Health	☒ YES ☐ NO	☐ YES ☒ NO	☒ YES ☐ NO		Dial 213-555-1212
EPA State	☒ YES ☐ NO	☐ YES ☒ NO	☒ YES ☐ NO		Dial 213-555-1212
Environmental Local	☒ YES ☐ NO	☐ YES ☒ NO	☐ YES ☒ NO		Dial 213-555-1212
Environmental	☒ YES ☐ NO	☐ YES ☒ NO	☐ YES ☒ NO		Dial 213-555-1212

Crisis Performance Score=14 | 0=Poor....18=Excellent | CM Capability Score=11

TP|PH|SY|Internal|Ext Stakeholders I|Ext Stakeholders II|Ext Stakeholders III

Return

Figure 5.20. Scores for external stakeholders.

INTERNAL STAKEHOLDERS

Stakeholders	Positive Role in Current Crisis?	CMT Training?	Member of CMT?	LOCATION	TELEPHONE #
?	☐ YES ☒ NO	☐ YES ☒ NO	☐ YES ☒ NO		Dial 213-555-1212
?	☐ YES ☒ NO	☐ YES ☒ NO	☐ YES ☒ NO		Dial 213-555-1212
?	☐ YES ☒ NO	☐ YES ☒ NO	☐ YES ☒ NO		Dial 213-555-1212
?	☐ YES ☒ NO	☐ YES ☒ NO	☐ YES ☒ NO		Dial 213-555-1212
?	☐ YES ☒ NO	☐ YES ☒ NO	☐ YES ☒ NO		Dial 213-555-1212
?	☐ YES ☒ NO	☐ YES ☒ NO	☐ YES ☒ NO		Dial 213-555-1212
?	☐ YES ☒ NO	☐ YES ☒ NO	☐ YES ☒ NO		Dial 213-555-1212
?	☐ YES ☒ NO	☐ YES ☒ NO	☐ YES ☒ NO		Dial 213-555-1212
?	☐ YES ☒ NO	☐ YES ☒ NO	☐ YES ☒ NO		Dial 213-555-1212

Return

External | More Internal

Figure 5.21. Where to list additional names and/or roles of members of your CMT.

151

If your computer is connected to a modem, you can also dial directly the person whose telephone number is to the extreme right of Figure 5.19, by clicking on the "Dial" button immediately to the left of the telephone number.

CM PROFILES

Once you have determined your CM Performance and Capability scores, click on the button "CM PRO-FILE" in Figure 5.14 to transfer you to Figure 5.22. Every time you arrive at Figure 5.22, the computer automatically checks whether your CM Performance or CM Capability scores have changed for any of the four main factors. The computer does this by comparing your new scores with your old scores, that is, the scores from the last time you arrived at Figure 5.22. If any of your scores have changed, the computer will automatically plot a new CM profile and record the time and the date of the new plot.

Figure 5.23 can also be reached from Figure 5.14, by clicking on the button with the arrow on the 5 in the box at the far left-hand side of Figure 5.14. Figure 5.24 can be reached from Figure 5.23 by click-

---

Figure 5.22. What you will see if you click on CM PROFILE in Figure 5.14.

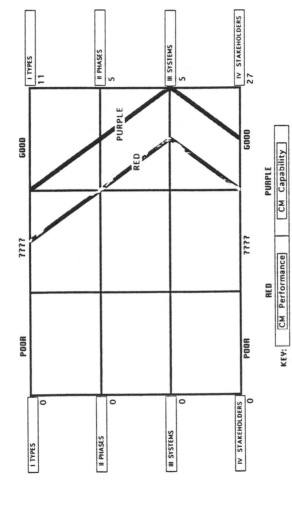

CM PROFILES

Today's Date= Thursday, June 16, 1994
Today's Time= 3:50:13 PM

Date of Graph= Wednesday, June 15,1994
Time of Graph= 1:56:20 PM

I TYPES		11
II PHASES		5
III SYSTEMS		5
IV STAKEHOLDERS		27

GOOD

PURPLE

RED

????

POOR

I TYPES	0
II PHASES	0
III SYSTEMS	0
IV STAKEHOLDERS	0

GOOD

????

POOR

RED   PURPLE

KEY: [CM Performance]   [CM Capability]

Note: If Only One Color Shows, Then The Two Profiles Are Identical.

[1st Card]   [AUDIT]   [QUIT]

153

DEVELOPMENT of CM CAPABILITIES

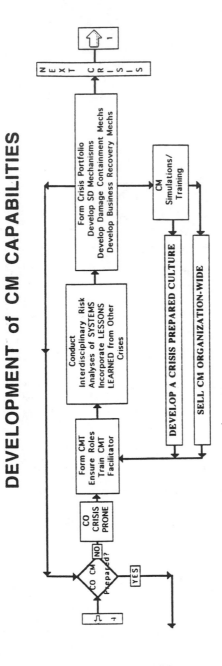

Figure 5.23. The development of CM capabilities.

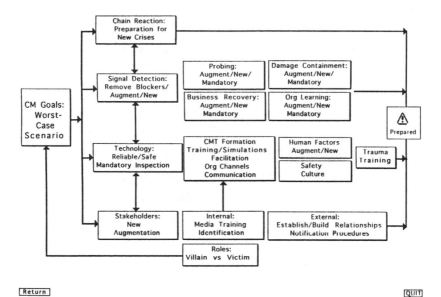

[Return]   [QUIT]

Figure 5.24. What you will see if you click on Conduct Interdisciplinary Risk Analyses . . . in Figure 5.23.

ing on the box "Conduct Interdisciplinary Risk Analyses . . ." in Figure 5.23. Clicking on "Return" in Figure 5.24 returns you to Figure 5.23. From Figure 5.23, you can go back to the first card by clicking on "1st Card," and so forth.

CONCLUDING REMARKS

The software program CrMgt described in this chapter is an integral part of the CM process. All fields, but especially new ones like CM, require all the tools they can muster to advance the state of the art. Indeed, we can say that a field will not truly begin to develop—let alone mature—until we have tools and frameworks to help assess its critical dimensions. Accordingly, we strongly urge you not to get caught up in the numbers of CrMgt for their own sake. All the numbers produced and used are no better than the judgments that created them. We especially recommend that you use CrMgt as part of a group process to allow the other members of the group—ideally, the members of your own organization's CMT—to express their opinions. This is the real purpose of CrMgt, to foster discussion and not to encourage entering meaningless numbers into a computer.

SIX

Managing Industrial Disasters

AN EXAMPLE

As we mentioned in the opening chapter, the decisions and activities required for effective CM can be generalized, regardless of the nature of the crisis. Chapters 2 and 5 presented a road map, or a visual crisis manual, of the entire CM process. That is, they laid out a broad set of actions and decisions that must be considered and perhaps taken, during the occurrence of a crisis. To understand the CM process even better, we shall apply in this chapter the framework to a specific crisis. This chapter discusses a contaminant leak, that is, a subtype of an industrial disaster. Our goal is not to supply a checklist for a particular type of crisis but to give you the opportunity to follow a detailed application of the CM approach we have developed.

A CRISIS SCENARIO

Assume you are the plant manager of a manufacturing company whose processes require the use of hazardous materials. Assume also that your plant is located in the Midwest near a river. The tasks required to process your products are, for the most part, predictable and simple. Your employees are loyal and enjoy stable employment and long tenure. First-line supervisors are often promoted directly from the ranks of workers. Middle managers come from two sources: plant veterans who have proved their commitment and value through the years, and management trainee-engineers who rotate jobs throughout the plant as part of their introduction to the organization.

Assume further, that it is 8:00 P.M. on a balmy Friday evening in late August. Because it is the end of summer, many of your employees are on vacation. Tonight, one of your best operations managers is acting as the plant manager. It is his phone call that will forestall your plans for a getaway weekend. On a routine inspection of the plant, the manager has smelled a "problem."

There seems to be a minor gas leak on the south side of the plant. The prevailing winds are from the north, and there are no residential communities within three miles south of the plant. The crew on duty quickly locates a small leak in one of the refrigeration components.

Let us stop the action for a moment and consider some of the CM plans and preparations that would be helpful in such a situation.

Goals

In the best possible case, the plant would be guided by goals and strategic guidelines that have been clearly and concisely articulated across the entire organization. These might include maintaining up-to-date training, tools, and equipment; preserving the employees' health and safety; and protecting the company's reputation. Although they may have seemed meaningless at the time they were formulated, they will be of critical help in determining your decisions and actions in the face of tonight's problems.

Guided by your general goals and guidelines and, further, as a manager in a CM-prepared organization, you are familiar with your company's strategic guidelines and priorities with regard to CM. After much deliberation, your CMT declares that your company will react positively, assume responsibility for resolving the problem, take into account environmental and public welfare, and maintain open communication with the media and relevant government agencies. This

solid underpinning enables you, and any other manager, to make decisions and take actions under extraor-
dinary conditions without having to wait for item-by-
item approval or specific executive guidance. As long
as you act within the established goals and guidelines,
you can be confident that your actions and decisions
will be supported by other company executives.

Signal Detection

Because your organization has invested time and
money in CM, it has well-established means of de-
tecting early warning signals of impending trouble.
In particular, your organization has a computerized,
companywide system for tracking crises, or near crises. In addition, all plant personnel have access to this
system. By tracking data from the entire company,
you can see whether signals from a variety of sources
point to a common problem. Without such a system,
individual, isolated signals may not "add up" to a
serious problem.

You take a quick look through the data. Nothing yet has been reported about a similar incident
since installing new equipment in the south building.
Nonetheless, the company's computer records make
available diagrams of the plant for locating and identifying potential sources of leaks. This information

proves especially useful to the maintenance supervisor on duty tonight because he has not had an opportunity to walk through the south building since the new equipment was installed. The computerized system thus enables him to isolate seventeen possible origins of the leak. As you continue to review the information at hand, you find the name and phone number of the subcontractor who last serviced the new equipment. A quick call to the subcontractor's night-shift troubleshooter helps your maintenance supervisor reduce the number of sources of the leak to three.

At this point, there is some uncertainty regarding the impact of the leak. You thus decide to notify the member of your corporate CMT who is on call for the weekend. You advise the executive of the current status of the plant, including questions remaining to be answered, as well as your projection of best- and worst-case scenarios. If the problem escalates to a full-blown crisis, you know that your corporate CMT will be able to provide immediate assistance by facilitating your access to critical resources. In addition, because of their broad experience with past incidents, the CMT could be useful resources themselves. The team represents such diverse departments as Operations, Government Affairs, Legal, Research and Engineering, Security, Maintenance, Environmental Health and Safety, and

Human Resources. By working together as a team, they have improved and sharpened their CM skills. Their primary objective in this kind of situation is to support your needs for managing a crisis in the field.

Preparation

If the incident erupts into a disaster, you know that there are well-developed and tested CM plans to handle it. You have already moved available experts into the plant's crisis ready room. Essential supplies, equipment, and communication links are located there in case they are needed. You know that CM plans, policies, and diagrams (such as those in Chapters 2 and 5) are available and up-to-date. In addition, the company has a policy of being proactive; that is, it continually tests and simulates emergency response plans. Furthermore, your plant has already exceeded the federal guidelines for health and safety compliance.

In the crisis ready room, you and other experts have immediate access to (and are familiar with) the CM plans as well as the site's specific procedures. A CM flowchart details the decisions and actions pertaining to plant leaks and explosions. You have already found the flowchart to be a convenient tracking aid, as well as a visual briefing tool, for those who continue to arrive on the scene. Although it now appears that the leak will not threaten the surrounding community, you are relieved to know that the plant has established and tested plans for alerting the neighborhood. If the incident worsens, your company even has specific guidelines for evacuating local residents and immediately providing them with support.

As part of its emphasis on crisis preparation, your corporate officers have encouraged the plant managers to know and be known in their communities. You have already made contact with regional, state, and national health authorities. The firefighters, police, and emergency response teams are familiar with the plant because they have been included in simulated crisis incidents. These sessions have given everyone the opportunity to evaluate the performance of various systems, to test the effectiveness of the plant's CM plans, and to make minor adjustments along the way. If the incident should get worse, you believe that the support you need will be there, and you can work as an expanded team because you already have had plenty of practice doing so.

Although you are skeptical about the corporate guidelines for open communication with the media, you find that they are paying off. Having been honest and forthcoming with the press when minor rumors circulated in the past, you find that the media are willing to neutralize coverage of the incident until you can give them more detailed information. You have made them comfortable in a temporary press room, and you have promised to fill in the details as soon as they are available.

Training

In the best possible case—long before a leak occurred or an incident threatened your manufacturing plant— you helped establish plans and mechanisms for responding to a crisis. These plans formed the groundwork for plantwide training. Having participated in several training sessions, you are confident that the plant's employees are experienced in responding to a crisis. They understand their own individual roles, as well as the importance of those roles in the plant's overall response plan. You have even had success recently in helping people understand that if they are not needed, they should stay away from the affected area. This has been a difficult task, as your employees generally care about the plant and one another and like to be in the center of action.

Let us return now to the crisis scenario. The acting plant manager has taken action in your absence, guided by the containment strategies that have been clearly described and, in most cases, practiced by the plant management team.

Containment and Response

At the first sign of a problem—whether it is the sounding of an alarm, a field report from an employee, or a call from the media, an activist group, or a member of the community (Table 6.1)—your

TABLE 6.1. SOURCES OF REPORTING OR ALLEGATIONS OF INDUSTRIAL ACCIDENTS

External	Internal
Complaint by community	Alert from Health and Safety Department
	Call from employee
Sounding of alarm	
	Field report from employee
Call from police	Call from Security Department
Call from media	Call from Public Affairs Department
Call from (state, federal) Health Department	
Call from hospital or doctor	
Call from saboteur	
Call from disgruntled employee	
Call from technical/ professional organizations	
Call from regulatory organizations	

primary role as acting manager is to begin gathering on-site information. To assess the plausibility and seriousness of the report, you try to determine what is known about the incident at hand:

1. Where in the plant can the leak have originated?

2. Who is available that is familiar with the plant and its operations?

3. What systems are in place to track or assess potential problems?

4. In regard to the potential for environmental contamination, what are the prevailing weather conditions?

5. How might this problem unfold over the next several hours (best-case and worst-case scenarios)?

6. How can the limited resources at hand be best deployed to deal with the current situation?

7. Who should be contacted inside and outside the company?

You are greatly relieved that all of your employees are accounted for, that no one was hurt. And there was no need for medical triage, although you were prepared to commence predesignated emergency procedures in case they were needed. You have given your local emergency medical services response team a call to stand by. You also have made sure that the equipment necessary for emergency communications is in place, and you have reviewed your evacuation procedures. Without any immediate threat to human health or safety, you continue to monitor the incident. You are confident that any health and safety needs can be met.

Business Resumption

Although the plant and the crew stood ready, you are relieved that there was no need to shut down the plant or the affected processes. The problem was resolved without slowing down operations, and there was no need to alter or discontinue production. With the assurance of your lead maintenance supervisor, you are glad to be able to notify the appropriate agencies and authorities that the problem has been fully resolved; in short, the leak has been fixed. Your next step is to notify the corporate CMT that the leak was found and repaired, there were no environmental effects on the surrounding area, and normal operations are continuing. You notify the CEO that he no longer needs to stand by as the company spokesman for the particular incident at hand.

With the incident under control, you go to the press briefing room, distribute a release, and carefully answer some questions. To alleviate any concerns, local radio and television reporters are notifying local residents of ongoing safety procedures.

Learning

Over the twelve years that you have been with the company, you have watched past incidents confirm the company's clear policy of "no-fault learning." Those involved in crises and near crises are encouraged to share pertinent information freely, knowing that they will not be punished for making honest mistakes. The company has always stressed that it is better to learn from mistakes than to point fingers in search of scapegoats.

Those involved in the incident (plant employees, managers, and corporate executives) will have an opportunity to describe their views regarding what might have gone wrong and what did go right. You pore through logs of activities surrounding the time of the incident. With the help of company experts, including personnel from other plants, you compare what happened with "normal" operating conditions in similar past incidents. In addition, experts from outside the organization who can provide additional information will be asked to give their opinions. When all the information has been collected, patterns will be identified in an attempt to learn what went well and what did not. As in the past, the emphasis throughout the entire process is on what can be done differently in the future to avoid similar occurrences and to make the plant even safer. Some of the lessons will be applied to modify existing CM plans and procedures so that future responses will be even better. Other lessons will be incorporated as minor changes in existing operating procedures. Plant employees will be notified of the improvements, and the lessons learned will be shared with sister plants throughout the organization.

A OVERVIEW OF CRISIS MANAGEMENT

Now that we have gone through the scenario and discussed the CM plans and procedures that a CM-prepared organization would have in place, let us review the case using the figures in Chapters 2 and 5 as a basis for analysis and comparison. In particular, Box 1 of Figure 2.1, the "starting point" of all crises, applies in the case of industrial accidents, but with some important modifications. From detailed studies of chemical plants, oil refineries, storage depots, and the like, the different sources of information typically associated with the reporting of industrial accidents or their allegation have been identified. This list (Table 6.1) is similar to Box 1, but with some differences.

By themselves, the various alarms/alerts/calls in Table 6.1 are insufficient to attract attention unless the organization also has mechanisms to receive and act on them. Consider, for instance, a disaster at New York's La Guardia and Kennedy airports a few years ago. Even though this was not strictly an industrial disaster, it contained features common to many industrial crises.

AT&T provides critical information to the air traffic controllers who operate La Guardia and Kennedy airports. In turn, AT&T obtains the electrical power it needs to run its computers and communication systems from Con Edison. At the peak of a summer heat wave, Con Ed experienced an unusual drop in power because of the added load due to the operation of so many air conditioners. As soon as the power dropped, AT&T's backup generators were programmed to begin operating, but the generators failed. A backup to the backup in the form of a single forty-eight-volt battery with a six-hour life then took over. As soon as the backup battery was activated, an alarm was sounded as a warning that the six-hour "clock" had begun. But this alarm was not heard until six and a half hours later. By this time, airplanes were circulating "blindly" in the air above La Guardia and Kennedy because the air traffic controllers could not land them safely. The point here is that the best alarms in the world are useless unless people can hear them, are motivated to do so, can immediately pass on the relevant information on to the right parties, and can take the appropriate actions. In examining the failure of its system, AT&T found that the operators who should have heard the alarm had been attending classes on a new backup system! Apparently no one had thought to leave at least one operator behind. This story indicates dramatically the tight interconnectedness among all the aspects of all the figures shown in Chapter 2, for example, between Points 1 (Figure 2.5) and 32 (Figure 2.7).

In another example, a large chemical plant had a pressure vessel that was controlled by a valve on one floor, but the gauge indicating the current level of pressure in the vessel was located on another. The operator literally had to run from one floor to the next in order to make changes in the pressure vessel and verify them!

Regardless of the source of a report of a potential industrial disaster (Table 6.1), crisis-prepared organizations should have established mechanisms in advance to route important calls to a central crisis command center. Thus in Figure 2.5, the arrow from Diamond 5 would be reversed to point upward, to show that crisis-prepared organizations treat incoming information differently than do crisis-unprepared or crisis-prone organizations.

Crisis-prepared organizations have operators who have been specially trained to handle important calls. They have been trained to listen calmly and empathetically, so that they can deal competently with the emotions and stress of crisis situations. They have specific forms and procedures to record important details and elicit information. For instance, they record the caller's tone of voice and general emotional state. They try to gather as many details as possible, such as (1) precisely what occurred, (2) when it occurred, (3) the full extent of injuries and damage, (4) the condition of surrounding roads and damage to equipment, and (5) the impact on the surrounding community. All such factors are used to assess the power and/or credibility of the source as well as to determine the position of the company in its response.

As a general rule, crisis-prepared organizations should be quick to begin fact-finding investigations and to clean up potential disaster sites. Thus at the first signs of a serious disaster (Diamond 2, Figure 2.5), they not only activate their CMT (Point 6) but also send a member from the CMT to the affected site so as to coordinate emergency treatment with on-site personnel.

Two sets of activities are initiated at (1) the corporate headquarters and (2) the affected site or sites. First, at the corporate headquarters, as soon as the CMT is activated, the availability of each of its members is ascertained, and their roles and the leaders are reassigned as appropriate. Second, the resources (medical treatment, supplies, and money) needed to treat the situation are checked.

At the site, three issues are paramount.

1. Has the situation caused significant contamination?
2. Does the contamination pose a serious health threat?
3. Is evacuation necessary?

If the answer to all three is yes, then a triage/evacuation should begin. But even if the answers to the first two questions are no, an evacuation may still be warranted if the public perceives the situation as hazardous. Even in such cases, however, the organization should still try to convince the public and the surrounding community that the situation is safe if the available medical, scientific, and technical information point to this conclusion. Nonetheless, the interaction with the community may have to proceed on grounds other than strictly "scientific." For example, the organization is advised to use spokespersons who have credibility with the community, who can speak in jargon-free terms. Unless this is done, all the best scientific data in the world may not be convincing and instead exacerbate the situation.

If an evacuation seems necessary, obviously, the most seriously injured should be treated and evacuated first. Next, the appropriate community emergency response groups should be notified. (This means that as part of being crisis prepared, the organization will already have established relationships with community response groups and relevant persons. It also means the organization will have shared its crisis response plans with those of the surrounding community organizations so that they can be coordinated.) Provisions for evacuating gawkers and preventing new ones from arriving at the scene must be coordinated and established.

One of the most important aspects of all crisis situations is the fact that they pose a threat to not only the physical condition of those persons and communities affected but also to their emotional state. Many organizations neglect the emotional and traumatic aspects of crises. Rather, specially trained workers should be involved who know how to listen and to elicit the feelings of those who have been touched by a crisis. Unless those concerned have a chance to express their feelings and emotions within the first forty-eight hours or so following a crisis, they will "clam up." But this does not mean that they will not be affected. Rather, they will be affected subconsciously in the forms of dreams, nightmares, and general anxiety.

If there have been serious injuries or deaths, the victims' families must be notified as quickly as possible. In many crisis situations, emotional harm has been compounded by delaying notification to families for days after a serious accident has occurred.

Prototype and protocol messages should be composed for the various media that will be interested in the details of the accident. The most general message that will serve the needs of diverse organizations should be well thought out. If the situation is extremely serious, the media will have to be managed with regard not only to the information given to them but crowd control as well.

It may be necessary to provide trauma treatment for those who have witnessed a crisis, as they can be affected emotionally as deeply as are those who experienced its direct effects. In addition, psychological support must be provided for those who have sustained serious injuries. In general, such support is part of the training of those who provide the emergency response. Finally, the senior managers and executives at the site should be not only treated but also informed of the full dimensions of the crisis and what is likely to follow in the days and weeks to come.

As we have emphasized throughout this book, the prompt and effective treatment of injured parties is the first concern of crisis-prepared organizations. In addition, many such organizations begin an accident investigation simultaneously with their treatment efforts. A basic question is whether the disaster had a natural or a human cause. Subsequent questions concern how the incident was handled. Whatever the causes, the appropriate authorities must be notified. The process of determining how and whether the incident occurred usually includes interviews with complainants, victims, witnesses, and coworkers.

There are several ways in which organizations can proceed through the figures in Chapters 2 and 5. As we emphasized earlier, the figures merely represent the most general CM processes and their relationships to one another. In most cases, organizations must attend to several critical features simultaneously; this is one of the main purposes of the figures, to show all the actions that must be considered so that you and your organization can initiate several lines of action and decision making simultaneously.

Once the treatment of affected persons is under way, and the causes of the situation have been assessed, the next critical phase of CM is resuming business and repairing critical operations. An important question is whether entire operations should be shut down. Do equipment and/or major processes have to be redesigned, or can you continue operations after they have been repaired? If critical equipment must be shut down or redesigned, additional actions will be necessary. These include notifying the proper federal and state authorities and insurance companies, coordinating and communicating with the designers of new technologies or identifying new technologies, assessing the public health impact of any new technologies, determining the amount of redesign required and the extent to which traditional production must be altered or discontinued, isolating those parts of the production processes that must be modified, and developing new plans for treating the broader environment affected by the disaster.

Many of these activities are contained in Figure 2.9, Diamond 44. But whereas the first set of treatment activities are those pertaining to the accident itself, a new set of evacuation and treatment strategies should be considered for the larger community, depending on the extent of the affected area. If a broader evacuation is required, many more coordinated activities must be undertaken. Federal and state agencies and authorities have to approve and coordinate evacuation plans and procedures. This may include the National Guard, the local police, and the Red Cross. Alternative evacuation sites must be established to treat people and to serve their long-term housing needs. In addition, communication strategies directing people to evacuate should be drawn up and transmitted by the appropriate media.

CONCLUDING REMARKS

As they apply to industrial accidents, Figures 2.5, 2.7, and 2.9 once again demonstrate the necessity of preparation. As part of their preparation, crisis-prepared organizations initiate the following activities before a crisis:

1. They designate and equip a crisis command center.
2. They offer media training to key managers and executives.
3. Their crisis plans incorporate the roles of the Operations, Personnel, Public Relations, Legal, and Financial departments.
4. They establish relationships with research and development/testing labs before an accident so that they can determine the causes and handling of a crisis.
5. They are proactive in forming, updating, and simulating the emergency response

plans and capabilities of critical operations.

6. They integrate the requirements of various government agencies in their crisis plans.

With regard to the last, this means that they integrate the testing methods, the response/operating procedures, the technical reporting/language requirements, and the health/human standards requirements as well.

In addition, crisis-prepared organizations draw up plans for alerting the surrounding communities. They establish means of securing community support, and they create communication linkages with important authorities and members of the community. They develop plans for obtaining firsthand information about the principal types of disasters. They contact "third parties" such as regional health authorities, national health authorities, state health authorities, local health authorities, regulatory agencies, law enforcement, industry associations, community emergency response groups, and nearby industries. They also develop plans to alert maintenance, the emergency response team, and security. They also ensure the availability of appropriate and adequate health and safety supplies and communication equipment.

Crisis-prepared organizations also regularly conduct "organizational climate/cultural surveys" to find out whether CM plans and procedures are taken seriously. They also establish accountability and rewards for crisis management in general and signal detection in particular. That is, they reward the behaviors they want to encourage, tying such rewards and recognition directly to signal detection preparation. They also make sure that their organizational structures are flexible so that they can shift quickly to the behaviors needed during a crisis. Finally, they practice simulations and training exercises to test their plans and procedures.

SEVEN

The Challenge
of Crisis Management

AN IDEAL CRISIS MANUAL

Despite all the attention given to crises in recent years, CM is still a newly emerging field. As a result, many of the concepts of CM are still neither well understood nor widely practiced by many organizations, even though hardly a month goes by without a crisis.

For example, on September 8, 1994, USAir Flight 427 crashed near Pittsburgh, killing all 132 passengers aboard. In reporting the tragedy, the media noted that this was the fifth USAir accident in five years and that more than 200 people had died. The fact that this was USAir's fifth accident in five years shaped the reporting of the tragedy from the very beginning. The natural question on most people's minds was whether the accidents followed a pattern. Were they independent of one another, as USAir executives claimed, or were they linked together in some way? Since USAir has been in financial trouble, did it knowingly cut back on critical maintenance, training, and service repairs? If it did not, could it prove that its maintenance, training, and service procedures were beyond reproach? Did its procedures meet or exceed mandated or industry standards?[1] Early reports also focused on the fact that the aircraft involved in the latest tragedy had had a history of minor problems (as most aircraft do), all of which had been "fixed" to government standards.

USAir's CEO appeared on a number of news media forums to rebut allegations that the separate accidents were somehow linked. In essence, he claimed that (1) there was no pattern, (2) the events were independent of one another, and (3) as testimony to his belief in the safety of USAir, he would have no qualms about any member of his family flying on any of his company's planes. But however well intentioned his statements were, his responses clearly revealed a lack of understanding of the fundamentals of CM.

In Figure 2.1, we indicated that the "power and/ or credibility" of the initial information source is one of the most important factors in exacerbating or squelching a crisis. Thus, the CEO's statements that he did not believe there was a pattern and that he would permit his family to fly on USAir may or may not have been believable to the general public. It is not clear whether these statements alone could establish his credibility (i.e., "He must be credible if he would allow his own family to fly on USAir") or whether they would be interpreted as self-serving and hence lower his credibility. In other words, it is not readily apparent whether his statements would either establish or detract from his credibility, because one must already have established credibility in order to be believed during a crisis.

This is not to say that one can never establish one's credibility during a crisis. Johnson & Johnson (J&J) not only established but even steadily increased its credibility during the Tylenol poisoning crisis,[2] by being completely candid. At one point, a top executive of J&J was asked by the press, "Can you eliminate entirely the possibility that the poisonings were done by someone on the inside?" The executive in charge said that he could eliminate the possibility of on-site poisoning because cyanide was not used in any of J&J's facilities. Later, however, this statement proved to be false. On learning that trace amounts of cyanide were used in one of J&J's facilities to test the quality of its products, the executive reconvened the press and stated, "I was wrong; we do have small amounts of cyanide in some of our testing labs; however, I can assure you that our cyanide was not responsible for the poisonings." By being absolutely candid with the press—including correcting himself when he was wrong—J&J's credibility was maintained throughout the tragedy.

What, then, might the USAir executives have done? First, we should acknowledge that questions of legal liability are present in every crisis, and so we must be extremely careful in commenting on any crisis. It is understandable that the airline executives wanted to avoid giving any credence to the perception that the accidents followed a pattern. Nonetheless, they must have known that this was precisely what the public feared. The trick, of course, is to address these fears without intensifying them, which is not easy. But unless this is done, people will probably feel that they are being patronized and that their fears are being dismissed.

OUTTHINKING THE UNTHINKABLE

One of the cardinal rules of CM is that public fears are not generally assuaged by "scientific facts or probabilities." Most people are not scientists or engineers, and so more often than not, they are highly skeptical of "experts." Accordingly, it would have been reasonable for USAir's CEO to have said something like "In my mind, I know that the separate incidents are not connected in any way. However, I can understand

and sympathize with those who feel that there could be such a pattern. As a result, I am ordering an immediate and thorough safety inspection of all our planes. We owe this to our passengers. In this way, we will make sure of the integrity of our planes and regain the trust and confidence of the public."[3]

Indeed, we are not recommending that USAir should have grounded its planes. Instead, our point is that such actions should at least be considered. For many organizations, a grounding or shutdown is probably as unthinkable as is the original crisis itself. But an unthinkable response may be the only effective counter. Whatever response is contemplated, it should be considered and evaluated in terms of Figures 2.5, 2.7, and 2.9.

CONCLUDING REMARKS

All the CM processes, charts, diagrams, and computer programs are useless unless your organization is ready to acknowledge that all crises create powerful emotions in those affected by them. We certainly hope that this book contributes to the technical knowledge and understanding of how to handle crises better. But this understanding alone is of little use unless organizations learn how to confront and overcome the patterns of denial that are generally present in a crisis, and such denial is the enemy of both handling the many details of CM and considering unthinkable actions.

In the end, therefore, CM is not solely a matter of better technical policies, procedures, and manuals. It depends critically on humans and organizations that are dedicated to facing reality.

POSTSCRIPT

Throughout this book, we have stressed the process of CM. For this reason, we have been extremely critical of most current CM manuals, because they generally ignore the broader process in which CM must be practiced. It is only fitting, therefore, that we present our ideal crisis manual after we have explained the process of CM.

Figure 7.1 shows the form of an ideal crisis manual. That is, each crisis that is included in an organization's crisis portfolio should ideally follow the form shown in Figure 7.1. In contrast, Figure 7.2 shows the form that most current CM manuals follow. An ideal crisis manual contains (1) the likely situations in which a crisis could occur, (2) those criteria that would have to be met or hurdles that would have to be exceeded in order for the organization to move into a crisis response mode, (3) the

Scenarios	Criteria	Signals	Containment	Recovery	Post-Crisis	Stakeholders
For each crisis family, at least one type of crisis that can occur and its root causes, ie, how, when, and why Likely versus worst-case scenarios, ie, worst possible time, circumstances, causes, and most unfavorable publicity	Criteria/ hurdles that must be surmounted to trigger a crisis response,(e.g. activation of the Crisis Management Team)	Early warning signals that a crisis is likely to occur, ie, events which are very near to the criteria	Physically isolate? Encase? Neutralize? Disperse? Treat? Physically remove? Transport? Reduce? Convert?	Prioritization of key customers Prioritization of key facilities manufacturing sites Backups for manufacturing information distribution Triage criteria	No-fault audit Review critique of key assumptions Causes? Key lessons learned vs not learned? Additional CMT training?	Prioritization of key stakeholders and their role in crisis plans/capabilities Contacts? Availability? Location? Part of CMT? Internal vs external?

Crisis Types	Audits	Meetings	Training	Miscellaneous
1. Criminal Attacks 2. Economic Attacks 3. Loss of Proprietary Information 4. Industrial Disaster 5. Natural Disaster 6. Equipment/Plant Malfunction 7. Legal 8. Perceptual/Reputational 9. HR/Occupational 10. Environmental/Health 11. Regulatory	Schedule of precrisis audits Scope of precrisis audits	CrisisMgtTeam Designer, operator, maintenance personnel Simulations Conflict mgt facilitator	CrisisMgtTeam Designer, operator, maintenance personnel Simulations Conflict mgt facilitator	This space is for recording miscellaneous information.

Figure 7.1. An ideal CM manual.

Containment	Recovery	Stakeholders
Physically isolate? Encase? Neutralize? Disperse? Treat? Physically Remove? Transport? Reduce? Convert?	Prioritization of key customers Prioritization of key facilities manufacturing sites Backups for manufacturing information distribution Triage criteria	Prioritization of key stakeholders and their role in crisis plans capabilities Contacts? Availability? Location? Part of CMT? Internal vs external?

Figure 7.2. A faulty CM manual.

signals indicating that the criteria in (2) are about to be met, (4) damage containment mechanisms or options, (5) recovery mechanisms and procedures, (6) postcrisis reviews, and (7) a list of relevant stakeholders. An ideal crisis manual also includes a history of pre- and postcrisis audits that have been performed, in order to assess the status and nature of the organization as a whole; a history of appropriate crisis management team meetings; and a history of training and simulations. Given our emphasis on the process of CM, the reader can appreciate why the ideal shown in Figure 7.1 differs substantially from that of most manuals in existence today (Figure 7.2).

Notes

1. An article in the *New York Times* challenged the adequacy of USAir's procedures and management structure. See Douglas Grantz and Ralph Blumenthal, "Troubles at USAir: Coincidence or More?" *New York Times*, November 13, 1994, pp. 1, 18, 19.

2. See Ian I. Mitroff and Ralph Kilmann, *Corporate Tragedies: Product Tampering, Sabotage, and Other Catastrophes* (New York: Praeger, 1984).

3. In "Troubles at USAir," Grantz and Blumenthal suggest that USAir "stand down" its management structure, not its planes.

INDEX

IIM (IAN I. MITROFF) LICENSE AGREEMENT

This is a legal agreement between you (either an individual or an entity), the end user, and IIM. If you do not agree to the terms of this Agreement, promptly return the disk to Oxford University Press, 198 Madison Ave., New York, New York 10016-4314.

IIM SOFTWARE LICENSE

(1) GRANT OF LICENSE. This IIM (Ian I. Mitroff) License Agreement ("License") permits you to use one copy of the specified version of the IIM software product identified below ("SOFTWARE") on any single computer provided SOFTWARE is in use on only one computer at any time unless you have express written permission from IIM, the author/developer of the SOFTWARE. The SOFTWARE is "in use" on a computer when it is loaded into the tem-

porary memory (i.e., RAM) or installed into the permanent memory (e.g., hard disk, CD-ROM, or other storage device) of that computer, except that a copy installed on a network server for the sole purpose of distribution to other computers is not "in use." If the anticipated number of users of the SOFTWARE will exceed the number of applicable Licenses, then you must have a reasonable mechanism or process in place to assure that the number of persons using the SOFTWARE concurrently does not exceed the number of Licenses. If the SOFTWARE is permanently installed on the hard disk or other storage device of the computer (other than a network server) and one person uses that computer more than eighty percent of the time it is in use, then that person may also use the SOFTWARE on a portable or home computer.

(2) COPYRIGHT. The SOFTWARE is owned by IIM and is protected by United States copyright laws in international treaty provisions. Therefore, you must treat the SOFTWARE like any other copyrighted material, e.g., a book or a musical recording, except that you may either (a) make one copy of the software solely for back up or archival purposes, or (b) transfer the SOFTWARE to a single hard disk provided you keep the original solely for back-up or archival purposes. You may not copy the written materials accompanying the SOFTWARE.

(3) OTHER RESTRICTIONS. This IIM License Agreement is your proof of license to exercise the rights granted herein and must be retained by you. You may not rent, lease, or transfer the SOFTWARE to other persons except that you transfer to another person on a permanent basis provided that you retain no copies and the recipient agrees to the terms of this license. You may not reverse engineer, decompile, or disassemble the SOFTWARE.

(4) LIMITED WARRANTY. IIM warrants that (a) the SOFTWARE will perform substantially in accordance with the accompanying written materials for a period of ninety (90) days from the date of receipt; and (b) any hardware accompanying the SOFTWARE will be free from defects in materials and workmanship under normal use and service for a period of one (1) year from the date of receipt. Any implied warranties on the SOFTWARE and hardware are limited to ninety (90) days and one (1) year, respectively.

(5) *NO OTHER WARRANTIES.* IIM disclaims all other warranties, either expressed or implied, including, but not limited to, implied warranties of merchantability and fitness for a particular purpose, with respect to the SOFTWARE, the accompanying written materials, and any accompanying hardware.

(6) *NO LIABILITY FOR CONSEQUENTIAL DAMAGES.* In no event shall IIM, Oxford University Press, or its suppliers be liable for any damages whatsoever (including, without limitation, damages for loss of business profits, business interruption, loss of business information, or other pecuniary loss) arising out of the use of or inability to use this IIM product, even if IIM has been advised of the possibility of such damages.

(7) The SOFTWARE was created on SuperCard. SuperCard is a registered trademark of the Allegiant Technology Corporation, Inc., copyright 1989–1991, 1994.